Where Is
NOAH'S
ARK?

Lloyd R. Bailey

festival books abingdon
NASHVILLE

WHERE IS NOAH'S ARK?

an original Festival paperback

Copyright © 1978 by Abingdon

ISBN 0-687-45039-4

MANUFACTURED IN THE UNITED STATES OF AMERICA

444649

For
Lloyd, Jr.
and
Ethan

May you combine love of Torah
with careful scholarship

Contents

1 Is There an Ark on Ararat? Some Preliminary Considerations

"ONE OF THE WORLD'S MOST PROVOCATIVE —and controversial—mysteries." Thus runs one enthusiastic description of the present-day search of Noah's ark.

From around the world, ark-searchers have converged on a rugged, remote section of Turkey, risking both life and the displeasure of the Turkish government, to ascend "Mount Ararat," where the remains of Noah's ark are considered to rest.

What have they found thus far? Is there an ark on Ararat—Noah's ark?

The belief that the great boat (ark) in which a family had escaped the waters of a worldwide flood could still be viewed at its original landing site began to be attested in the Near East in the late pre-Christian period. Reports of its survival continued through the Middle Ages and have intensified in the Christian West in the last century. Within the last two decades a number of books have appeared, some of them best sellers, offering detailed reasons for believing, not only that the ark of Noah had survived relatively intact atop a mountain in eastern Turkey, but that parts of it had been recovered and were on display in France. A large number of articles concerning this matter have appeared in newspapers (e.g., *New York Times, Grit*), magazines (e.g., *Life, Reader's Digest*), and religious publications (e.g., *Christian Century*). Even wider interest has been generated by a number of movies, one of which was recently shown on prime-time network television (*In Search of Noah's Ark*, NBC, May 2 and Dec. 24, 1977). It probably is safe to say that there are few persons in the United States who are unaware of this topic.

Some of those who are actively involved in the search for the ark have, with a mixture of humor and seriousness, coined the term "arkeology" to describe their activity, and they have organized a number of expeditions to the upper reaches of "Mount Ararat." This mountain, which they believe to satisfy the geographical requirements of Genesis 8:4, is a spectacular 16,950-foot peak near the Turkish border with Russia and Iran. It is called Büyük ("Big") Ağri Daği (or Dağ) by the Turks [pronounced: ärï däï], Jabal al-Harith by the Muslim historians, and Masis by the ancient Armenians.[1]

Evidence for the ark's survival, as presented in the various popular publications and movies, usually is of four types: (1) ancient reports that it could still be seen, beginning as early as the third century, B.C., and continuing thereafter in Jewish, Christian, and Muslim sources; (2) modern eye-witness accounts that an intact wooden structure stands at the snow line on "Mount Ararat" (at about 13,500 feet), and that its dimensions agree with the biblical description of Noah's ark; (3) photographs, allegedly showing a boat-shaped structure said to be located high on the mountain, taken from the ground, from aircraft, and by satellite; (4) hand-hewn beams said to have been recovered from beneath a glacier at the snow line and to have been assigned an age of five thousand years by supposedly reputable agencies, thus allowing the beams to be old enough to meet the requirements of a literal biblical chronology for the flood.

While this topic has understandably caught the popular interest, biblical scholars at major academic institutions have almost totally ignored it. Consequently, there is scarcely a source to which interested persons can go for an informed, calm, nonpolemical investigation of the claims that are being made. It is crucial that such an investigation be undertaken, since some of the books by ark-searchers (a term which I will use hereafter instead of "arkeologist") are flawed by misunderstandings and misuse of the ancient sources, the use of "evidence" that most other investigators have discredited, and a failure to investigate the accuracy of some of the tests used to arrive at an age of five thousand years for the "ark wood." It is also obvious that some of the ark-searchers seem to have made up their minds prior to an objective examination of the evidence.

Among the questions that must be asked concerning the claim that parts of the ark have been recovered from "Mount Ararat" are the following:

1. The ark came to rest upon "the mountains of Ararat." First of all, where is "Ararat"? Is the "Mount Ararat" which is the focus of modern investigation (Buyuk Agri Dagi) the same site as indicated in Genesis 8:4? Do the early reports of the

9

ark's survival all point to the same site? How many Noah's arks have been discovered, and where?

2. What do the ancient reports say? Do they all deal with the biblical Noah? Have any of the writers personally seen the remains? Is the mentality and world-view of the ancient reporters so congenial with our own that their word can be accepted without question?

3. Are the recent eye-witness accounts in general agreement? Are the witnesses still living so that they may authenticate the stories attributed to them? If some of them been exposed as fabrications? How not, have the stories been reliably transmitted? Have well do their details accord with the known geography of the mountain?

4. Are the objects in the photos undeniably a boat, or is there disagreement? Are all of the photos genuine? *additional*

5. How reliable are the testing methods that resulted in an age determination of five thousand years? Are all the results in agreement? Has evidence appeared since the last popular presentation, that is, since the movie?

6. If there is a wooden structure of considerable age near the top of Buyuk Agri Dagi, is it automatically to be acknowledged as Noah's ark? Are there reasonable options to this conclusion? What ancient reports are there of other structures on this mountain?

7. How might a massive structure, regardless of its nature, have gotten to such a difficult height? Since there are no trees on Buyuk Agri Dagi, should one reasonably conclude that the heavy timbers must

have floated there from a great distance? What do we know about the mountain in antiquity? Was it always barren?

Certain other questions have deliberately been set aside in this inquiry, not because I find them uninteresting, but because I find them unnecessary and because I suspect that they would be divisive. (1) To what extent is the Genesis flood narrative historical? Do we interpret it literally, or how? Does it describe a local, or a universal, flood? (2) Is a universal flood possible, geologically and meteorologically? From where would all the water have come, and where could it have gone thereafter? Whatever the reader's conclusions about these matters, they need not enter into the subject that we are about to investigate. They may predispose one's hearing of the evidence, and they can affect one's willingness to listen to the case being presented ("you can't trust that book, because it's author does/does not believe so-and-so"). As far as the present volume is concerned, the reader may believe or not believe the literal historicity of the Genesis account, according to preference. The issue is, instead, simply this: either the reported sightings and photographs are creditable evidence, or they are not; either the wood offered in evidence is of sufficient age to meet the specifications of a literal biblical chronology for the flood, or it is not.

It must be emphasized that, should the evidence presented in previous books and movies fail to withstand scrutiny, it would not indicate that the biblical flood narrative is unhistorical. Conversely, if the evidence does withstand scrutiny, it would not prove the accuracy of that narrative. An ancient wooden structure high on a mountain in Turkey, even if boat-shaped and five thousand years old, is not *automatically* to be associated with the biblical Noah.

Finally, the reader must realize that this volume is hardly the last word on the topic. Indeed, it is merely a beginning. A thorough, definitive investigation would require years, vast sums of money, and expertise in a great many disciplines (biblical studies; analysis of still more documents in Armenian, Arabic, and Byzantine Greek; knowledge of the geological history of northeastern Turkey; an acquaintance with wood chemistry, physics, and dendrochronology; and several others). My resources and abilities in some of these areas have been limited, as readers will doubtless be aware. I trust, however, that it will be a worthwhile contribution to the continuing debate.

2 Where in the World Is Ararat?

THE ARK, SAYS THE WRITER OF GENESIS, came to rest "upon the *mountains* of Ararat." Presumably we have on the best evidence (it says so in the Bible) a definite landing place for Noah's ark. But note that there are several mountains involved; "Mount Ararat" as such never appears in the Bible.

Problems arise immediately, however, when we ask "*Where* was Ararat?" What did the biblical writers have in mind by the term? Is there any way we today can discover just what they meant? Fortunately, we can get some clues. Genesis 8:4 is the only place in the Bible where the landing place of the ark is mentioned, and it is clear that an individual peak is not singled out. This is in agreement with other biblical writers, who use the term "Ararat" to indicate a considerably larger area. The assassins of Sennacherib, king of Assyria, flee northward from Mesopotamia to "the *land* of Ararat" (II Kings 19:37; Isa. 37:38). Jeremiah summons *"kingdoms"* from the north for war against the Babylonians: "Ararat, Minni, and Ashkenaz" (51:27).

Ararat would thus seem to be a mountainous area of some extent, a political "kingdom" north of Mesopotamia, bordering the ancient lands of Minni and Ashkenaz. A precise location cannot easily be

13

assigned to Ashkenaz. Its people seem to have been nomadic Scythians from beyond the Caucasus Mountains who settled in the plain of the Araxes River and northward. But the Kingdom of Minni is known from Assyrian records (where it is called Manna) to have been southeast of Lake Urmia. Thus, the Kingdom of Ararat likely would be located between Assyria and Minni, somewhere around Lakes Van and Urmia in modern Turkey.

Ararat is itself mentioned in Assyrian records, where it is called Urartu. In the thirteenth century, B.C. Shalmaneser I uses this term to refer to a group of small kingdoms located southeast of Lake Van. Twelfth-century records (Tiglath-pileser I) refer to a kingdom west of the lake as Nairi; by the ninth century this Nairi has been incorporated into Urartu. Thus the boundaries of the Kingdom of Urartu became, generally: the Euphrates River on the west, the crest of the western Taurus Mountains on the south; and the borders with the Kingdom of Manna in the upper reaches of the Zagros Mountains to the southeast of Lake Urmia. The northern boundary is uncertain, but it may have extended to the plain of the Araxes River. It is clear that political concentration was in the vicinity of Lake Van where the capital, Tushpa, was located[1] (see maps IA and IB).

During a period of military strength in the ninth and eighth centuries, the kings of Urartu were able to expand their borders westward across the Euphrates and southward into Syria as far as Aleppo. During this time, the term "Ararat" could be used to indi-

MAP IA

**Boundaries of the
Kingdom of Urartu**

Where is Noah's Ark?

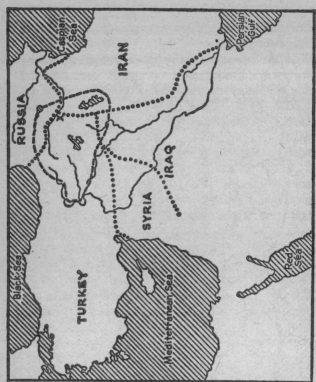

MAP 1B

The Kingdom of Urartu (Ararat)
In relation to modern boundaries

•••••••••• modern boundary

------- boundary of Urartu

x location of Agri Dagi
("Mount Ararat")

cate almost the entire mountainous district north of Syro-Mesopotamia.

In the late eighth century the Assyrians, led by Sargon II, invaded the heartland of Urartu/Ararat and plundered its cities. It was then invaded by no-madic tribesmen from across the Caucasus Moun-tains, the Cimmerians and Scythians, in the seventh century, and finally destroyed by the Medes in the early sixth century.

As we can now see, the Genesis flood narrative is not very specific about the ark's landing place. "The mountains of Ararat" seems to refer not to a moun-tain peak but a mountainous kingdom. How then did the tradition develop that the ark had come to rest upon a specific peak? Possibly through a mis-reading of Genesis 8:4, so that it becomes "Mount Ararat" rather than the "mountains of Ararat." To this must be added the understandable human de-sire to locate holy places as precisely as possible (for example, some persons seek the exact spot where Jesus was born, tried, crucified, and buried).

Ararat Become Armenia

The Armenians, mentioned as early as the Behis-tun inscription of Darius I of Persia (522–486 B.C.), may have migrated to the Urartu/Ararat area from Phrygia.[2] Their first settlement seems to have been at the headwaters of the river Halys, and Herodotus, in the fifth century, B.C. clearly distinguishes them from part of the older population which he calls Alarodians. (His "Alarod" seems to be a linguistic variation of Ararat/d[3].) As the new Armenian popu-lation moved east and north, the Alarodians (Araratians) were increasingly pushed toward the plain of the Araxes.[4] This situation is reflected in the administrative divisions of the Persian Empire: the thirteenth satrapy (a political area) included the Armenians and had its capital at the city of Van, just east of the lake, while the eighteenth included the Alarodians and was situated to the northeast on the Araxes.[5] Thereafter, Ararat (called Airarat by the Armenians) became just a northerly subdivision of the Arsacid Kingdom of Armenia (during the second and third centuries, A.D.).[6] Thus Jerome in the fourth century A.D. can remark, commenting on Isaiah 37:38, "Ararat is a region in Armenia on the Araxis . . . at the foot of the great Taurus Mountain."[7]

Around the beginning of the Christian era, readers of Genesis would probably understand the word "Ararat" in terms of the geography of their own day, rather than that of the Genesis narrator. That is, they might restrict the term to the small district on the Araxes, the Ararat of their time, rather than properly equating it with the much larger ancient Kingdom of Urartu. The result would be that one tall mountain in this area, Agri Dagi, rising dramatically from the plain of the Araxes, would become a prime candidate for Mount Ararat.

Many of the earliest translations of the Bible, done in the centuries just before and after the beginning of the Christian era, render the term "Ararat" as "Armenia."[8] This was entirely proper, since the Armenia of the translators' day was roughly equivalent in size to the ancient Kingdom of Urartu/ Ararat. The area had gained a measure of independence in the early second century, B.C., and was divided into Greater and Lesser Armenia. The former extended eastward as far as the Caspian Sea and northward to the river Cyrus; the latter extended westward to the River Halys (see map II). After 80 B.C., Greater Armenia sometimes expanded southward to include an area along the Tigris River, an area called Qardu by the Semites, and Gordyene (Gordyaea) by the Greeks and Romans.[9] It is in this mountainous area (Qardu/Gordyene), in the extreme south of Ararat/Armenia, that ancient tradition will locate *another* possibility for the ark's landing place (see chap. 3).

While Armenia was a country of considerable size and with fluctuating boundaries, its religious and administrative center was to the north in the Airarat district, on the Araxes River, centering in the cities of Armavir and Artaxata (Artashat). Indeed, Armenian tradition stressed that Haik, the ancestor of the entire group, had first settled in this very area. Thus, even the term "Armenia," when encountered in the early translations of the Genesis flood story, might suggest more to some readers than Greater Armenia. It could be taken to mean Armenia par excellence, the heartland on the Araxes. If so, then the ark's landing place ("in the mountains of Armenia") would again be restricted to a narrow area, and again one mountain, Agri Dagi, would become a prime candidate.

But here it must be stressed that even some of the early translations of the Bible, for example, the Syriac Peshitta and the Aramaic Targums, understand the word "Ararat" in the wide sense, and translate it

19

in a way that exempts Agri Dagi as the prime candidate for the ark's landing place. These translations say that the ark landed "in the Qardu (Gordyene) Mountains," south and east of Lakes Van and Urmia, but still within the boundaries of Ararat.

Conclusions

1. During the period when the traditions in Genesis took their final shape, the term "Ararat" meant a rather extensive area with slightly fluctuating boundaries. This area can be equated with the Kingdom of Urartu, known from Assyrian records. In general, the Kingdom of Urartu was concentrated in the extensive Qardu/Gordyene Mountains around Lakes Van and Urmia.

2. No one mountain is singled out in the Genesis account as the ark's landing place. Rather, a mountainous area is specified, and this is a more apt description of the Qardu area (where the Taurus and Zagros ranges collide) than of the more northerly valley of the River Araxes where Agri Dagi is located. Hence some of the ancient translations of the Bible translate "mountains of Ararat" by "mountains of Qardu."

3. By the beginning of the Christian Era, the boundaries of Armenia were roughly those of ancient Ararat/Urartu, so that some translations of Genesis justifiably read that the ark came to rest in "the mountains of Armenia." But the phrase "mountains of Ararat," found in the Hebrew original and in some other ancient translations, might lead to a misunderstanding. By then, Ararat was only a small, northerly district of Armenia. Undue

emphasis might then be placed on the possibility that the ark landed in the north, in the vicinity of Agri Dagi.

4. By the time of the conversion of Armenia to Christianity (fourth century) and the introduction of an alphabet, so that the Bible could be translated into Armenian (fifth century), Armenia was a semi-independent kingdom whose religious and administrative centers were concentrated in the northern part of the country.[10] Thus when some persons read in the early translations that the ark had come to rest in "the mountains of Armenia," and when Armenians in particular read this in their own Bible, they might understand it in a much more restricted sense than the writer of Genesis intended. Attention would be focused too narrowly toward the north where Agri Dagi was located.

Our study thus far has not enabled us to decide whether the authors of the Genesis flood story had a specific site in mind when they referred to the mountains of Ararat. But it has (a) helped to establish the geographical boundaries within which specific sites could legitimately be proposed; (b) indicated the plausibility of a southern location, that is, in the Qardu (Gordyene) Mountains, as suggested by some ancient translations; and (c) given some of the reasons why a specific mountain farther to the north, Agri Dagi, would later be singled out by some people as the landing place of Noah's ark.

3 Other Mountains, Other Arks Ancient Reports of the Ark's Survival

IT IS A VERY NATURAL HUMAN DESIRE TO want to locate—and visit—historic and holy places. Throughout the centuries men and women have made pilgrimages, paid fees, to see the "place where it happened."

Although, as we have seen in the last chapter, the Bible does not specify the exact landing place of Noah's ark (nor does it make any mention of the ark surviving), natural human curiosity has led to a wide variety of proposals. Particularly during the Byzantine Era were there ark speculations and searches.[1] The fact that there are many proposed ark landing sites is often ignored by some modern-day ark-searchers, who indiscriminately gather all ancient reports and present them as if every mention of Mount Ararat automatically meant Agri Dagi.

Often-Discussed Landing Sites

1. **Jabal Judi,** in the Arabian Peninsula (see map II) is mentioned in the Koran (11:44). It is located in the 'Aja' Range, whose peaks rise almost perpendicularly to a height of 5,600 feet from the edges of the great Nafud Desert in the Najd,[2] and it was famous for its pre-Islamic temples.[3] The Muslims may have picked up the ark tradition for this mountain from Syrian Christians, since Bishop

MAP II

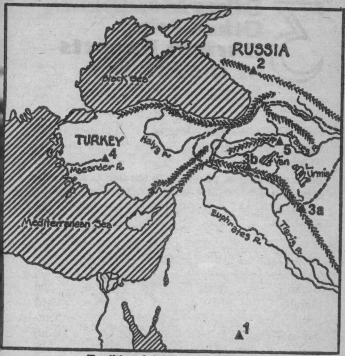

Traditional Ark Landing Sites

mountain range ≫≫≫≫

boundary of Armenia, 1st cent. B.C.–1st cent. A.D. ----------
Armenia Minor to the West (between the Halys and Euphrates)

mountains or areas identified as the landing place of the ark
  1. Jabal (Mount) Jūdī
  2. Mount Baris (?)
3a. in Adiabene
3b. in Gordyene (later called Jabal Jūdī)
  4. near Celaenae
  5. Buyuk Agri Dagi (Masis: "Mount Ararat")

Where is Noah's Ark?

Theophilus of Antioch (second century) reports, "The remains of the ark are to be seen in the Arabian mountains to this day."[4] It is possible, however, that Theophilus is referring to Arabia Deserta (which extended to the upper limits of the Mesopotamian plain) rather than Arabia Felix (Arabia proper), and if so he would be referring to the Qardu Mountains just beyond the Tigris (see site 3b, map II). In any case, the tradition still survives in Arabia, since,

> In the town of Chenna, in Arabia Felix, says the traveller Prèvoux, is a large building, said to have been erected by Noah; and a large piece of wood is exhibited through an iron grating, which is said to have formed a portion of his ark.[5]

Muslim tradition includes the belief that the ark sailed seven times around the Kaaba in Mecca before traveling on to its final resting-place.

2. **Mount Baris**, "above Minyas in Armenia, where, as the story goes, many refugees found safety at the time of the flood, and one man, transported upon an ark, grounded upon the summit, and relics of the timber were for long preserved; this might well be the same man of whom Moses, the Jewish legislator, wrote."[6] Mount Baris is not otherwise mentioned in ancient records, and the location of Minyas is uncertain.[7] In any case, there is no real reason to identify it with Mount Ararat (Agri Dagi). Indeed, one may wonder if Mount Baris might be Mount Elbruz, the highest peak of the Caucasus range, 18,465 feet tall, and at the northern limit of Armenia.[8] The identification of Mount Elbruz with Baris is perhaps strengthened

by a similar tradition, which is still current in Armenia,[9] that Noah and his family were not the only survivors of the flood. While his ark rested on Agri Dagi, other persons had climbed to the top of a still higher mountain *to the north* which remained above the waters.

3. Somewhere in the mountains of modern Kurdistan (the upper Zagros range, northeast of Mesopotamia), with the possibility that more than one site is indicated.

(3a) In Adiabene—roughly between the Upper and Lower Zab Rivers, tributaries of the Tigris (see map II). In the first century A.D. Josephus, discussing the royal family at Adiabene, remarks, "[in] a district called Carra [Carron][10] . . . the remains of the ark in which report has it that Noah was saved from the flood . . . to this day are shown to those who are curious to see them."[11] In the third century Hippolytus wrote: "The relics of this ark are . . . shown to this day in the mountains called Ararat, which are situated in the direction of the country of the Adiabene."[12] And possibly Julius Africanus, also writing in the third century, has this location in mind: "And the ark settled on the mountains of Ararat, which we know to be in Parthia."[13] This site may be the same as that of the Gilgamesh Epic (11:140), where Utnapishtim's boat comes to rest on Mount Nisir, which is likely the spectacular Pir Omar Gudrun (called Pira Magrun by the Kurds), just south of the Lower Zab River.[14]

(3b) In Gordyene (Gordyaea), the mountainous area between the Tigris and the Upper Zab rivers, south and southeast of Lake Van (see map

II). Thus Strabo, after having discussed the city of Nisibis in upper Mesopotamia, says: "Near the Tigris lie the places belonging to the Gordyaeans, whom the ancients called Karduchians; . . . [they were] held in subjection by the king of the Armenians."[15]

This area is called Qardu(n) in Aramaic and Syriac sources; "the mountains of the Karduchi" by Xenophon;[16] and "the Gordian Mountains" by Ptolemy.[17] It was part of the Armenian province of Korcaik (Gord-Haïk) and particularly of the Canton called Gordouk (see below, site 5, and maps III and IV). It is part of the area still known as Kurdistan. (Note that the sounds g, k, and q, are easily interchanged in the languages of this area.)

Several of the Targums (Aramaic translations of the Bible: Onkelos, Neofiti, and Pseudo-Jonathan A) render the "mountains of Ararat" in Genesis 8:4 as the "mountains of Qardu(n)," as do the Peshitta (the Syriac Bible) and other Jewish and Christian sources.[18]

The idea that Noah's ark landed in this area may come from Berossus, a Babylonian writer of the third century B.C., who, telling how the ancient Sumerian flood-hero Ziusudra survived the deluge, says: "There is still some part of the ship [of Ziusudra] in Armenia, at the mountain of the Gordyaeans; and some people carry off pieces of the bitumen . . . and use (it) as amulets." Josephus, who quotes these remarks,[19] happily identifies Ziusudra with the biblical Noah and does not seem to remember that he has located the ark in two or three different places (sites 2 and 3a). It may be,

MAP III

Provinces of Armenia in the 5th cent. A.D. (based upon H. Hübschmann, "Die altarmenischen Ortsnamen," in *Indogermanische Forschungen* 16.

● Nisibis
▲ Jabal Jūdī
■ Buyuk Agri Dagi

1. Upper Armenia (Barjr-Haïk)
2. Fourth Armenia (Corrord-Haïk)
3. Aljnik (Arzanene)
4. Turuberan (Taraun)
5. Mokk
6. Korčaik (Gord-Haïk; Gordyene)
7. Persian Armenia (Parska-Haïk)
8. Vaspurakan
9. Siunik (Sisagan)
10. Arçex
11. Inner Armenia (Phaïtakaran)
12. Uti
13. Gugark (Gogarene)
14. Taik
15. Araŗat

27

however, that the adjoining territories, Adiabene and Gordyene, were roughly the same in his mind, as indeed they were to others. For example, Pliny[20] places Nisibis in Adiabene. Less excusable are modern ark-searchers who quote Berossus as if he supported their view that the ark had landed on Agri Dagi—site 5, map II.

Theophilus of Antioch may have had this location in mind when he mentions that the ark came to rest in the Arabian Mountains (see site 1, above).

Epiphanius, Bishop of Salamis, in the fourth century, trying to make it clear that Gordyene falls within the area of biblical Ararat/Armenia, reports that the ark rested "in the mountains of Ararat, [i.e.,] in the midst of [the mountains of] Armenia and [of] Gordyene."[21] An alternative translation might be, "between the mountains of Armenia and those of Gordyene," in which case he might be trying to harmonize the geographical terms. In another passage, however, Epiphanius says unambiguously that "the remains of Noah's ark are still shown in the land of the Gordians."[22]

An attempt to harmonize the various traditions seems to be the reason for Targum Jonathan's explanation of Genesis 8:4. This translation suggests that the mountain had two peaks. The ark came to rest "on the mountains of Qardun [Gordyene]: the name of the one mountain is Qardunia, and the name of the other mountain is Armenia."

The Nestorian (Syriac-speaking) Christians put the specific landing place on a conspicuous mountain that rises just north of the Tigris at the edge of the Gordvene/Oardu range: a 6,800-foot peak, now called by the Turks Cudi Dag. (It may have been called Mount Nipur by the Assyrians,[23] and perhaps revered by them, since King Sennacherib carved massive reliefs there about the year 700 B.C.)[24] The Nestorians built several monasteries on the mountain, including one on the summit called the Cloister of the Ark. This was destroyed by lightning in A.D. 766.[25]

The Muslims, who conquered this area in the seventh century, A.D., accepted the Nestorian tradition of the ark's landing on Cudi Dag and erected a mosque on the site of the Cloister of the Ark. Several explanations have been offered for the fact that they came to call this mountain Jabal Judi, thereby creating confusion with site 1, above. (1) The Assyrians had called this area the land of Guti (Kutu), and that terminology may have survived as Judi until the Islamic period.[26] (2) Judi/Cudi is a corruption of Gardu/Qardu, i.e., the consonant r has been lost.[27] (3) The name has been transferred from the Jabal Judi in Arabia (site 1, above),[28] earlier believed to be the landing place.

During the early Islamic period, Jews, Christians, and Muslims are in general agreement that this mountain is the ark's landing place:

"The ark rested on the mountains of Ararat, that is, Jabal Judi near Mosul." —Eutychius, Bishop of Alexandria [Sa'id ibn-Bitrik] (ninth century).[29]

"The ark came to rest on Jabal Judi . . . 8 parasangs from the Tigris. The place . . . is still to be seen." —al-Mas'ūdi (tenth century).[30]

Where is Noah's Ark?

"[I travelled] two days to Jezireh Ben 'Omar, an island in the Tigris, on the foot of Mount Ararat . . . on which the ark of Noah rested. 'Omar Ben al-Khatab removed the ark from the summit of the two mountains and made a mosque of it." —Benjamin of Tudela (twelfth century).[31]

"In order to see the place where the ark landed, he [the Emperor Heraclius, seventh century] climbed Jabal Judi, which overlooks all the land thereabout." —al-Makin (thirteenth century).[32]

That wood said to have come from the ark was recovered from atop the mountain—indeed that a Muslim sanctuary had been constructed there from it—is reported in the thirteenth century by the Muslim geographer Zakariya ben Muhammad al-Kazwine.[33]

On the slopes of the mountain there was, according to the ancient sources, a village called Themanin, meaning in Syriac "Eighty": "And when they came out of the ark, they built themselves a city and called it Themanin, according to their number, for they said, 'We are eight.' "[34] Again, "Judi is a mountain, near Nisibis. . . . At the foot of it there is a village called Themabin; and they say that the companions of Noah descended here from the ark, and built this village."[35] The village is now called Betmanim, or Heshtan.[36] According to the biblical account, the ark contained eight persons: Noah, his wife, their three sons, and their wives. In Nestorian Christian and Muslim tradition, the eight (*themane*) has become confused with eighty (*themanin*), giving rise to the tradition that Noah's family was accompanied by a group of persons, totaling eighty.

Relatively recent visitors to the mountain report that the ruins of the Nestorian monasteries are still visible, as well as a structure (mostly of stone) called Sefinet Nebi Nuh ("the Ship of Noah").[37] Annually, on September 14, representatives of all faiths in the area—Christians, Jews, Muslims, Sabians, Yezidis—gather to commemorate Noah's first sacrifice atop the mountain.[38]

There is still one other ancient attestation to the Gordian/Qardu Mountains as the ark's landing place, although previous books by ark-searchers have failed to realize it: Faustus of Byzantium's (see site 5).

4. Near **Celaenae in Phrygia**. This location seems to reflect the combining of Semitic and Greek flood stories. Julius Africanus, after giving his own opinion (3*a*, above), mentions that others prefer this location. It is also mentioned in the Sibylline Oracles (200 B.C.–A.D. 500): "There is in Phrygia . . . a steep tall mountain, Ararat . . . thence streams of the great River Marsyas spring . . . there . . . the ark [of Noah] abode."[39] At the nearby city of Apamea,[40] also called Cibotus (κιβωτός—"box; ark"?—in any case, it is the term used in the Bible for Noah's ark; but the meaning could be something like "Treasury"),[41] coins of the fourth century A.D. were struck apparently depicting this scene. A couple seem to be looking out a window of a boat; another couple is outside. There are two birds, one approaching the boat with a tree branch in its claws, and an inscription on the side of the boat reads ΝΩΕ ("Noah"?).

31

Today's "Mount Ararat"

5. Agrī Dagi (Büyük Ağri Daği; Masis in Armenian) is the Mount Ararat of present-day arksearchers. Armenian tradition has placed a number of Noah-related stories in the vicinity of this spectacular mountain: the Garden of Eden; Noah's first grapevine (still bearing fruit until it was destroyed in the earthquake of A.D. 1840); the burial place of his wife (at Murand) and of Noah himself (at Nakhichavan); the spot where he first stepped from the ark; the location of his house.[42] Most important and basic to all of the above traditions is the claim that his ark came to rest on the mountain and that *it survives there largely intact to this day*. While few persons would doubt that these traditions have grown over the centuries and that some of them are less than historical (the grapevine and the burial places are certainly doubtful), the idea that this is the genuine landing place of the historical Noah has recently been ardently proclaimed.

By now it should be clear that traditions from the

ancient Near East are not unanimous in saying
where the flood-hero's boat landed. The accounts
examined thus far that specifically mention Noah are
either very general as to location (for example, in
the mountains of Ararat/Armenia, a vast area with
several possible locations) or seem to point to specific mountains other than Agri Dagi. Thus the basic
question becomes: How old is the tradition that says
Noah's ark landed atop this majestic peak?

An attempt to trace it to the first century A.D. is
made by quoting Josephus: "The ark rested on the
top of a certain mountain in Armenia . . . both he
[Noah] and his family went out . . . the Armenians
call this place 'The Place of Descent' ('Αποβατήριον)
. . . the remains of the ark are shown by the inhabitants to this day."[43] While Josephus is thus not very
specific, his translator William Whiston (A.D. 1737),
in a clumsily worded note, seems to identify this
"place of descent" with a city at the foot of Agri
Dagi: Ptolemy's Naxuana,[44] Moses of Chorene's
Idsheuan, and modern Nachidsheuan (i.e., Nakhichevan in the U.S.S.R., which name, he says, means
"the *first* place of descent"). The problems with
Whiston's often-quoted identification are several and
serious.

(1) Josephus here merely uses the general term
"Armenia." Elsewhere (sites 3*a, b,* above,) he has
more specifically placed the landing site in that part
of Armenia called Adiabene or Gordyene (Qardu),
far removed from Agri Dagi, and there is nothing
in the present passage to contradict this.

(2) Just as several of the traditional locations
have recently yielded wood that has been taken as

evidence to support the claim (sites 1, 3*b*, 5), we need not be surprised if more than one of them, indeed each of them, included a spot formally named "The Place of Descent." Thus the same name found in Josephus and in the vicinity of Agri Dagi would not prove that Josephus was referring to the latter.

(3) Since a variety of ark traditions that originated at other locations have been transferred to Agri Dagi (see below), it is possible that this one originated elsewhere as well. Indeed, the Armenians may have borrowed it from Josephus' account, since his works were translated into Armenian in the fifth century A.D.

(4) There are two cities named Idchavan (= Whiston's Idsheuan?) in Armenia: one in the Province of Taik, the other in the Province of Airarat, whereas Nakhichevan is in the Province of Vaspurakan.[45] Thus the two names cannot refer to the same place.

(5) Moses of Chorene, at least in his *History*, does not even mention a place called Idsheuan.[46]

(6) There is a controversy surrounding the date of Moses and his various writings. His *History* is an account of his native Armenia from its legendary beginnings down to the year A.D. 440 and dedicated to Prince Isaac, who died in 481. Understandably, therefore, he has traditionally been dated to the fifth century. However, modern critical studies have seriously undermined that date, as well as his accuracy as a historian.[47] Specifically, the work seems to refer to a number of events that happened much later, most of them in the sixth and seventh centuries

34

(e.g., the provincial divisions made by Justinian in A.D. 536, and the monastery of Zwartnots, which was not built until 654). The problem seems resolved to the extent that experts in the field have recently confined their debate almost entirely to whether Moses' work is to be assigned to the eighth or even the late ninth century.[48] The very existence of the scholarly debate is often ignored by popular writers who are out to prove that the ark survives atop Agri Dagi.[49] Matters are not helped by the fact that the debate is often printed in hard-to-obtain sources and in such languages as Armenian and Russian.

(7) Early Armenian tradition does not identify the landing place with Agri Dagi, but rather with the Gordyene/Qardu Mountains far to the south. For example, in an eighth-century account, King Tiridates ascends to the summit to get stones with which to build a chapel. There is no indication that the mountain should not be climbed or that an angel was thought to guard anything, to say nothing of the ark! (See Appendix II.)

(8) The earliest form of the place-name "Nachidsheuan" is Naxcavan, which, contrary to the often-quoted opinion of Whiston, does *not* mean "the place of first descent" and thus can not be equated with anything in Josephus' text! Rather, the name consists of a place name, *Naxč* (or *Naxuč*) plus *avan*, "market town." See Appendix I.

Since the last two points are crucial for rejecting the claim that Josephus' remarks support Agri Dagi as the ark's landing place, it is necessary that they be developed in greater detail. The relevant information can be found in a little known article, written in German seventy-five years ago by a respected grammarian of the Armenian language, H. Hübschmann. An English translation of this article is given in Appendix I. Now, however, another claim must be considered.

Faustus of Byzantium is sometimes cited as a fifth-century, A.D. witness that Agri Dagi was the ark's landing place.[50] He related that St. Jacob (or James), Bishop of Nisibis (modern Nusaybin) on the river Habur in upper Mesopotamia, desired to see the ark. "[He] left his village and journeyed to Mt. Sararad[51] in the Armenian Mountains in the region of Airaratic control (domain) in the Canton of Gordukh. . . . Having arrived, he asked God to let him see the preserved ark that Noah had built, which had come to rest on this mountain at the time of the deluge" (*History*, III.10). After a difficult climb, he fell asleep near the summit, only to be awakened by an angel who informed him that it was not God's will that he ascend higher. In compensation for not being allowed to see the ark, he was given a small piece of it, "which is preserved to this day."[52]

Concerning Faustus' report, ark-searchers would do well to ponder these points:

(1) Had he meant to refer to Agri Dagi, he presumably would have used its well-known Armenian name, Masis, as he does elsewhere (for example, at III.20).

(2) He uses the unique expression, "in the region of Airaratic control," which is *not* the same as the Province of Airarat (he uses the latter term

at III.7, 12, 14; IV.24; V.6; VI.1, 6) where Agri Dagi is located.

(3) Faustus specifically places the mountain in "the Canton of Gordukh." A canton is a smaller division of a province, and it is agreed by writers ancient and modern that Gordukh lies in the Province of Korcaik[53] (Gord-Haik; Gordjaik: see map III), that is, in the mountainous area between the Tigris and Lake Van,[54] the same area which Semitic writers call Qardu and which classical writers call Gordyene (see map II). Indeed, Gordukh is the canton nearest the Tigris and thus almost within sight of St. Jacob's hometown of Nisibis (see map IV). This is clear not only from Armenian sources but from Muslim geographers who relate that the Canton of Bakarda (or Kardai), which is the Armenian Gordukh, included the city of Jazirat ibn 'Omar, located on an island in the Tigris![55] It is quite clear, then, that Faustus' mountain is far removed from Agri Dagi in the Province of Airarat. Rather, it should be identified with Jabal Judi in Gordyene (site 3b, above).

Furthermore, Ptolemy, in his *Geography*, separates the area in which Agri Dagi is located from the Gordian Mountains by 3 degrees latitude,[56] which, in his system of reckoning, is a distance of 150 miles! The city of Naxuana, which Whiston sought to identify with Josephus' 'Αποβατήριον and with Armenian "Nachidsheuan," is separated by the same distance from the Gordian Mountains.

Ark-searcher John Montgomery, who argues that Agri Dagi is the landing place, avoids this fatal testimony from Faustus and Ptolemy, and indeed uses them to support his position. He, apparently mistak-

Where is Noah's Ark?

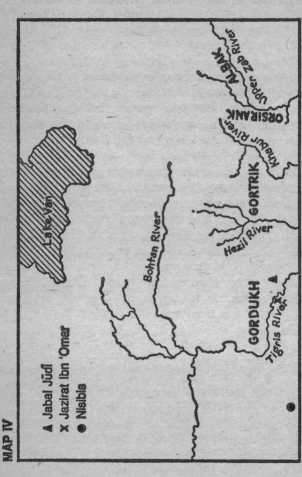

MAP IV

▲ Jabal Jūdī
× Jazirat Ibn 'Omar
● Nisibis

Lake Van

Bohtan River

Hezil River

Tigris River

Khabur River

Upper Zab River

ALBAK

ORSIRANK

GORTRIK

GORDUKH

Cantons of the Province of Korčaik (Gord-Haïk; Gordyene)
in the 5th cent. A.D. (based upon H. Hübschmann in *Indogermanische Forschungen XVI*)

enly, assumes that Faustus' reference to Airarat means the province; he identifies Faustus "Gordukh" with a "Cortaea" in Ptolemy, said to be mentioned at *Geography*, V. 13.[57] Unfortunately, however, I can not find a place named "Cortaea" in critical editions of Ptolemy's Greek text.[58] It presumably is a misreading[59] from a Latin translation, either of "Coriaea"[60] or of "Cotaea."[61] Cotaea is at the same latitude as the Gordyene Mountains, and Coriaea is one degree even further *south*, and so both are totally unrelated to Agri Dagi.

Faustus' account is evaluated in the article by Hübschmann (see Appendix I). Hübschmann's conclusion is that the older Armenian writers all understood the Gordian (Qardu) Mountains to be the ark's landing place. This was true of Faustus as well. Only after the eleventh/twelfth century A.D. was the location shifted to Agri Dagi. Thereafter, the name of the nearby city Naxcavan ("Naxcville") was reinterpreted to mean "the first settling place" (Naxijavan or Nachidscheuan).

Hübschmann does not exhaust the evidence that the original geographical setting of Faustus' story was the Gordian/Qardu Mountains, perhaps Jabal Judi in particular. Additional information seems to support that conclusion.

(1) People who still live in the vicinity of Jabal Judi tell a story that is very similar to the adventure of St. Jacob. A holy man had vowed to visit the remains of the ark on Jabal Judi, but he was discouraged by an evil spirit who gave him the false report that the summit was still a month's journey ahead.[62]

Where is Noah's Ark?

(2) It would certainly be surprising if the Syrian St. Jacob, resident of Nisibis and thus within sight of the Qardu Mountains—the very range which the Bible, in the local Aramaic and Syriac translations, indicated as the ark's landing place—ignored that area and journeyed instead to the edge of the known world. Had he done so, he would have been denying the traditions and indeed the scriptures of his community, a community that he served as bishop.

(3) St. Ephraem the Syrian (Ephraem Syrus), described as Jacob's student and life-long companion, several times refers to the resting-place of Noah's ark as "the mountains of Qardu."[63] If Jacob had set out to find the ark on Agri Dagi, and if his belief had been confirmed by an angel, it is scarcely believable that Ephraem would have ignored all this and continued to proclaim that the ark was nearby in the Qardu Mountains.

(4) Bar-Hebraeus, the revered Syriac theologian and philosopher (1226–1286) who lived in this same area, would presumably have been aware of a successful journey which Bishop Jacob had taken to Agri Dagi to recover the ark. Yet he continued to affirm that the landing place was Mount Qardu![64]

By the twelfth century, however, it is clear that many Armenians had come to assume that Faustus' story was about an area near Agri Dagi. For example, there is the report of Vincent of Beauvais:

Mount Arach, where Noah's ark rests, . . . (is near) the river Arathosi [Araxes], which . . . empties into the Caspian Sea. . . . It is said that no man has ever ascended it, except for one monk. . . .

When he had climbed part of the way, he would
fall asleep. . . . Finally, however, the Lord gave in
to his persistence. . . . When he returned he brought
one of the beams from the Ark back with him.[65]

The description of the surrounding territory suggests that the Arakad Mountains (Mt. Aragats;
Ala-Göz), 12,000 feet high and perpetually snow
covered, are meant. A hermitage (named Hreshta-
kabnak, "House of the Angel") on the flank claims
to possess a fragment of the ark and the hand of St.
Jacob. (See Appendix II.) It is a mistake, therefore,
to emend Vincent's text from "Arach" to "Ararat"
as is commonly done (e.g., by Montgomery, *Quest,*
p. 81).

What brought about this transfer of Faustus' story
from Jabal Judi to Arach, and then to Agri Dagi?
We can make a few educated guesses.

(1) Faustus' "region of Airaratic control" could
be taken, erroneously, to indicate the Province of
Airarat on the Araxes, in which Agri Dagi was located.

(2) The spread of Christianity to upper Armenia, attributed to St. Gregory the Illuminator,[66]
was assisted by St. Jacob, who sent there a large
shipment of his own writings.[67] Perhaps among the
material sent was the story of Jacob's search for the
ark on Mount Ararat, which, to local ears, would
suggest the nearby province of that name. If so, the
identification of the mountain with the spectacular
Agri Dagi would be pretty much a matter of course.

(3) The city of Jazirat ibn Omar, at the foot of
Jabal Judi, had close commercial ties with the in-
terior of Armenia.[68] Thus there would be plenty of

opportunity for stories to be transferred from one place to the other by caravaneers.

Such a transference of stories and legends would also have been greatly assisted by the geographical factors outlined in chapter 2—particularly, the shrinking of the ancient Kingdom of Ararat (Urartu) to a small province (Airarat) in the north; the fact that the heart of Armenia was located in the Araxes plain.

Such transfer of traditions to Agri Dagi can be illustrated from sources other than Faustus. For example, Keryat Themanin ("the Village of the Eighty," originally "Eight": see site 3b, above), located on the flank of Jabal Judi, was, according to Christian and Muslim traditions, founded by Noah. At least by the thirteenth century, the tradition has been transferred to Agri Dagi—with the Semitic name of the town intact. William of Roubruck reports:

> Near this city [of Naxua] are mountains in which they say that Noah's ark rests; and there are two mountains, the one greater than the other; and the Araxes flows at their base; and there is a town there called Cemanum, which interpreted means "eight," and they say that it was thus called from the eight persons who came out of the ark, and who built it on the greater mountain.[69]

The 80/8 variation occurs at both locations, supporting the dependence of one story upon the other.

Agri Dagi and Jabal Judi have other ark traditions in common—although which ones derived from the other (if any) is not so evident. For example, it was said that the ark, floating north, temporarily came to rest on a peak, then journeyed on to its final resting place. In the case of Jabal Judi, the ark stopped first at Jabal Sinjar;[70] on its way to Agri Dagi it stopped at Suphan Dag.

In addition, it should be noted that both mountains were the site of monasteries connected with the ark story (St. Jacob and St. Gregory on Agri Dagi; the Cloister of the Ark, and others, on Jabal Judi)[71] and that the grave of Noah is shown near the foot of each.[72]

Other Sites of Ark-Landings

6. The Book of Jubilees (second century B.C.) mentions one. "And the ark went and rested on the top of Lubar, one of the mountains of Ararat" (5:28; cf. 7:1; 10:15). Since Jubilees sometimes supplies names for places that are left nameless in the Bible, we cannot be sure that, in geography of its time, there was a specific peak called Lubar, and if so, where it was located. Epiphanius, however, continuing in a passage cited above (site 3b), assigns a location: the ark came to rest "in the mountains of Ararat, in the midst of (or, "in between") the mountains of Armenia and of Kurdistan [Gordyene], on a mountain called Lubar." There is a real possibility that he is merely combining various names or locations rather than relating personal knowledge of a mountain by this name. The same designation is mentioned in Jewish midrashic literature[73] and in the Byzantine historians Georgius

Cedrenus in the eleventh century and Georgius Syncellus in the ninth century.[74]

The possibility that the word "Lubar" might be related either to the word "baris" or to "Elbruz" (site 2, above) has been noted in passing by a few scholars.[75]

7. According to Samaritan tradition (but not in the Samaritan translation of the Bible), the ark landed in Ceylon, or Serandib. In Islamic tradition as well, a number of biblical episodes are localized in Ceylon.[76]

8. One tradition locates the ark in Persia (modern Iran). It was said to have landed on Alwand (Elwand) Kuh, an 11,700-foot peak in the Zagros range near Ecbatana (Hamadhan), which is also connected with Paradise.[77] A map in Calmet's *Dictionnaire historique de la Bible* (1722), shows the ark atop this mountain (?), which it calls "Mont Ararat." Another tradition points to Mount Demavand, a spectacular 19,000-foot peak in the Elburz range just south of the Caspian Sea. Jews living in this area trace their ancestry back to the exiles who were settled there by Shalmaneser of Assyria (II Kings 17:6).[78] Some modern scholars identify Nicolas of Damascus' "Mount Baris" (above, site 2) with this mountain.[79]

It should be added that Persians who live in the vicinity of Agri Dagi accept it as the ark's landing site, calling it Kuh-i-Nuh ("The Mountain of Noah").

9. A few nineteenth-century scholars locate the ark in Afghanistan—in Hindu Cush, an offshoot of the Parmir-Himalaya Range.[80]

Summary and Conclusions

1. Which one of the various landing places mentioned in ancient sources is the "correct" one? At present, any answer is pure guesswork. The biblical writer does not name a specific site; rather, a vast geographical area is given (Ararat/Urartu), within which several of the proposed sites fall. If the matter is ever to be decided definitely, it will have to be by means other than the ancient reports.

2. Many of the ancient sources not only say that the ark has survived to the present; they also introduce wood from the ark as evidence. Thus, such claims for Agri Dagi (or any other site) are not unique; indeed, they are precisely what we would expect.

3. None of the ancient writers claims to have seen the ark or any part of it, or to have visited a landing site—or even to have conversed directly with anyone who has. They only quote someone else, usually ending with the cliché, "It is said that the remains of the ark are to be seen to this day." This they report, even if centuries have passed since the original source.

4. Various groups, believing their area to have been the cradle of civilization, or the center of the earth, point to the most conspicuous mountain in the vicinity as the ark's landing place. For some Arabs in the Arabian Peninsula, it would be Jabal Judi in the 'Aja' range (site 1); for Jews in Babylonia, Mount Nisir (?) in the Zagros (site 3a); for Jews and Christians in upper Mesopotamia, Jabal Judi in the Gordian/Qardu Mountains (site 3b). In

Armenia, after the introduction of Christianity and the translation of the Bible into Armenian, it would be Arach or the spectacular Masis—Agri Dagi.

5. Among these ancient traditions, the one associated with Agri Dagi seems to be very late—likely the latest, since it dates to the eleventh/twelfth centuries at the earliest.

In sum: While the ancient reports are interesting and point to literary and archaeological phenomena that merit further investigation, they are not, within themselves, convincing evidence that the ark has survived. Less problematic evidence will need to be produced, as even ark-searchers admit: "The total number of such accounts does not overly impress the researcher; and by no means do these accounts provide conclusive proof that the Ark has survived."[81]

4 I Found It! Some Recent Eyewitness Accounts of the Ark

THOSE WHO SET OUT TO CONQUER AGRI Dagi had to face a fearsome climb—snowstorms, winds, poisonous snakes, treacherous footing were just a few of the hazards. In addition, there was the local Armenian belief that a terrible demon lurked on the upper heights. It is hardly surprising, therefore, that a firm conviction grew up that no one could reach the summit.[1]

Thus from the Middle Ages until comparatively recent times, we have only the hearsay kind of ark evidence that the ancient reports contained. "But at the summit a great black object is always visible, which is said to be the Ark of Noah" (Jehan Haithron, thirteenth century). "Near this city [of Naxua] are mountains in which they say that Noah's ark rests" (William of Roubruck, thirteenth century). "The Armenians . . . are of the opinion that there are still upon the said mountain some remainders of the ark. . . ." (Adam Olearius, seventeenth century). "Twelve leagues to the east of Erivan one sees the famous mountain where almost everyone agrees that Noah's ark landed—though no one offers solid proof of it" (John Chardin, seventeenth century).[2]

During the eighteenth century, such "it-is-reported" evidence was not good enough apparently. John

Warwick Montgomery remarks: "Not surprisingly, the 18th-century age of 'Enlightenment' provides no additional accounts of Ark sightings: the rationalists and deists of the time were not inclined to seek confirmation of biblical revelation in scientific and historical matters."[3] But such an evaluation of the silence is hardly to the point, since the Bible itself makes no claim that the ark survived, even briefly—to say nothing of claiming that it landed on Agri Dagi.

The first verifiable ascent to the summit was made in the year 1829, by J. J. Friedrich Parrot and a company of five other persons.[4] Soon thereafter, the old hearsay evidence is replaced by direct, eye-witness accounts. It is claimed that the severe earthquakes that shook the mountain in 1840[5] and in 1883 exposed Noah's ark, which previously had been largely hidden beneath the ice cap.[6]

The case for the ark's survival, as presented in current books and movies, depends heavily upon the eye-witness accounts. Unlike the ancient reports, there is no doubt as to which mountain is meant. Instead of "a great black object" seen from a distance, the claim is now made that the ark has actually been touched, entered, and explored and that it accords exactly with the description in Genesis. It is imperative, therefore, that such accounts be both taken seriously and scrutinized carefully. Some of the more famous ones will be outlined below, followed by brief observations. (It must be emphasized that I have not interviewed persons or sought to verify the existence of the documents alleged to contain eye-witness accounts. I am, rather, dependent upon the accounts as they are given in books authored by ark-searchers.)

The Account of the Old Armenian

First is the strange story attributed to an Armenian Seventh-Day Adventist, Haji Yearam, related in his seventy-fifth year after a near-fatal illness. As a youth (about 1856?) he and his father had guided "three vile men who did not believe the Bible" to the intact ark high on Agri Dagi. It had several floors and contained animal cages with the bars still in place. The men, enraged that the Bible thus appeared to be vindicated, tried to destroy the structure but found that they could not do so. It was too massive; the wood had become "more like stone than any wood" and could not be burned. Thereupon they descended the mountain, threatening their guides with torture and murder should they ever reveal what had been found.

Harold Williams, who cared for Yearam during his illness, says that about 1918, near the time of Yearam's death, he saw a newspaper report of the death of an "elderly scientist" in England. The scientists had confessed, just before dying, that he had participated in an adventure identical to that related by Yearam. And thus the account of the ark's discovery would seem to be verified in a remarkable and unquestionable fashion.[7]

The following curiosities about this story should be noted: (1) Williams apparently made little mention of Yearam's adventure until 1952—remarkable in view of the sensational nature of the case. (2) Williams' report is prefaced by a troublesome "If I remember correctly . . ." (3) Where would the "vile" scientists have learned of the ark's location? Known written reports are confined to obscure seventeenth-century (or earlier) travelers. Would English scientists be moved to undertake such a lengthy and hazardous journey to combat such hearsay evidence? Although there was a British expedition to the mountain in 1856, it cannot be connected with Yearam's three "scientists." It was a company of five, led by Major Robert Stuart. They were guided up the mountain by Kurds, not Armenians, and had no interest in trying to find the ark.[8] (4) The reason for guiding the westerners up the mountain, put in the mouth of Yearam's father, sounds precisely, and surprisingly, like the thought of modern American ark-searchers. It goes something like this: "God had hidden the ark until now, but the time has come to confound unbelievers." Does this suggest that Yearam's story has been embellished as it was retold? If so, to what extent? (5) The ark was described as covered with "varnish or lacquer," a curious state of affairs for wood long aged by the elements of nature. This sounds more like a subsequent attempt to explain why the wood had survived than an accurate, on-the-spot observation. In any case, other eye-witnesses have described the wood as covered with moss (Hagopian) or as very soft (Bryce). (6) Why would the men have tried to silence their guides, when apparently the location of the ark was already well known, especially to the inhabitants of the area? Or why would they think that a family in remote Armenia would have such access to western news media that the episode would become known? (7) Yearam died in 1920 at the age of eighty-two.[9] The scientist, who was "much older than he," allegedly told the story about the same time, so he must have been over a hundred years old. (8) The scientists have never been identified, nor has a copy of the newspaper which Williams quotes ever been produced, despite a diligent search.

Bryce's Wood

In 1876 the Englishman James Bryce found a timber at the 13,000-foot level, "about four feet long and five inches thick, evidently cut by some tool."[10] It was easy to cut (in contrast to the reports of Yearam and others), and he severed a piece of it with his ice-axe and carried it away. Bryce, a careful observer, considered it possibly to be a part of Noah's ark, and his account is often published in support of the ark's survival. However, in a seldom-quoted passage, he reflects: "I am, however, bound to admit that another explanation of the presence of this piece of timber . . . did occur to me. But as no man is bound to discredit his own relic, . . . I will not disturb my readers' minds, or yield to the rationalizing tendencies of the age by suggesting it."[11]

The Turkish Expedition

An article in the British newspaper *Prophetic Messenger*, dated 1883, is said to quote a news release from Turkey: a governmental expedition, sent to survey the damage to Agri Dagi caused by an earthquake, found a portion of the ark projecting from a glacier. It was forty to fifty feet in height, and contained compartments about twelve to fifteen feet in height.[12]

The report is remarkable for at least the following reasons. (1) In order to reach the heights of the mountain, the groups went through a "dense forest." This is in absolute contrast to many detailed descriptions of the mountain, which report that there are no trees at all—to say nothing of a dense forest![13] (2) The group also encountered a stream on the mountain, "wading sometimes waist high in water." Other accounts mention occasional streams from the melting snow of the glacier, but otherwise there is usually no flowing water on the mountain.[14] (3) Despite the great age of the wood and the fact that it was "painted . . . with a dark brown pigment," the visitors recognized the species of tree and pronounced it identical with the gopher wood of the Genesis account. This easy identification is in contrast to the later case of Fernand Navarra (see chap. 6), whose wood specimens could not be identified with absolute certainty even by the wood scientists who examined it. And as for the biblical "gopher wood," its species remains a mystery. (4) The original news release, cited by the *Prophetic Messenger*, has never been produced. (5) The story seems to have gathered additional details as it spread from newspaper to newspaper, with the *Prophetic Messenger* version representing a late stage of development. In an earlier report, in a Dutch newspaper dated July 28, 1883, we reportedly read only that the ark has been found in Armenia in a well-preserved state, that it is made of "gopher wood," and that an American had already made an offer to purchase it.[15]

52

Prince John Joseph

John Joseph, sometimes identified as "Prince of Nouri," "Grand-Archdeacon of Babylon," and "Episcopal Head of the Nestorian Church of Malabar, South India," claims to be another witness. In 1887, after three (or eight, according to some accounts) attempts, he claims to have reached the top of Agri Dagi and found the ark. He entered the structure, which projected from beneath ice and snow, and made detailed measurements which coincided exactly, so he said, with the dimensions of the ark in Genesis. His grand scheme to remove the ark and take it to the Chicago World's Fair of 1893 did not materialize.[16]

The problems with this account include: (1) He reported that the beams of the structure were joined "with long nails." This detail is emphatically denied by others who claim to have been inside the same ark (Hagopian). (2) He was, it seems, unable to verify any of his pretentious titles. Although he was apparently refused ordination as bishop by the Nestorian Patriarch, he continued, for at least ten years, to announce that he was on his way to the ordination service.[17] (3) At public lectures he was unable to convince others of the truth of his claim (even his close friends said that he "almost convinced others"). (4) We are told on the one hand that he indeed gained the backing of "Belgian financiers" for his plan to relocate the ark but that the Turkish government refused permission; and on the other hand that he was unable to secure such backing.[18] (5) Since the length of a cubit (Gen. 6:15) is not precisely known,[19] it is curious that the dimensions

53

of the structure on the mountain "coincided exactly" with the biblical description. In any case, since the structure was not totally exposed ("wedged in the rocks and half-filled with snow and ice"), one wonders how the measurements were possible. (6) He reportedly was a mental patient at the State Institution in Napa, California.[20] I have written to the hospital's director for confirmation of this claim, but he refused to respond on the ground that the confidentiality of records is protected by state law.

Another Elderly Armenian

An elderly Armenian immigrant to the U.S., Georgie Hagopian, reported that at the age of ten he was taken to the ark by his uncle, around 1902.[21] His observations, based upon two hours of exploring the ark, include: it was a thousand feet long, six to seven hundred feet wide, and maybe forty feet high; the wood was so hard that a bullet would not penetrate it; it was joined with wooden dowels, with no nails in evidence; no doors were visible, but one could ascend to the top by means of a ladder.

The following discrepancies with other accounts are immediately evident; (1) Others found the wood easy to cut (Navarra, Bryce, Knight); (2) Nouri observed that it was joined with nails, not dowels. Since both he and Hagopian claim to have spent hours inside the structure, such a difference can hardly be attributed to faulty observation or poor memory. (3) Previous visitors found a massive door laying beside the ark (Yearam) or entered through a hole in the side (the governmental expedition of 1883). (4) The dimensions are possibly

54

twice those of Genesis, and thus twice the size of Nouri's find.

The Russian Aviator

Perhaps the most celebrated sighting is attributed to a Russian aviator named Roskovitsky, who allegedly photographed the ark from the air in 1917. An expedition later allegedly made detailed measurements and photographs. All these documents, however, are said to have perished in the Russian Revolution. According to published accounts —which curiously did not appear until 1940, and then in a magazine entitled *New Eden,* published in Los Angeles—the ark was spotted on the shore of a lake, with about one fourth of its length beached. A catwalk was visible down its length. The ground expedition found hundreds of small rooms, some with cages made of iron bars. Nearby was a small shrine at which Noah had offered his sacrifice after leaving the ark.

Even ardent ark-searchers now admit that this story is almost entirely fiction, including the name Roskovitsky.[22] Apparently, however, there is a historical nucleus to the story, which has been related by relatives of now deceased Russian soldiers of the expedition. From the air, something was spotted in a lake; a ground party could not reach a wooden structure in a swamp because of snakes. But unfortunately for even this alleged nucleus, no one has yet been able to authenticate such terrain on the mountain; indeed, all geographical knowledge contradicts it. The only known swamps on Agri Dagi are at the foot of the mountain. As for the alleged cages made of iron, it is necessary to remember that this metal was discovered by the Hittites about 1500 B.C., far too late for use in Noah's ark.

Knight's Expedition

New Zealander Hardwicke Knight found huge timbers projecting from beneath glacial ice in 1936. He "broke off" a piece of wood, which was quite soggy, and carried it away. It deteriorated rapidly.[23] The contrast between the condition of this wood and all the previous specimens should be immediately obvious.

The Kurdish Farmer

A Kurdish farmer named Resit is reported to have discovered the ark in 1948.[24] The prow, "about the size of a house," was projecting from beneath the ice "about 2/3 of the way up" the mountain. Its wood, blackened with age, was so hard that a piece of it could not be severed with a knife. Resit's fellow villagers, upon hearing his account, climbed to the site and agreed that it was unmistakenly a boat.

The account, reportedly carried by the Associated Press,[25] motivated A. J. Smith, dean of a small Bible college in North Carolina, to journey to the mountain in 1949. His goal was to locate Resit, hire him to serve as a guide, and verify that the ark had at last been discovered. Unfortunately, however, Resit could not be found. A search of villages "for 100 miles around" failed to produce anyone who claimed ever to have seen the ark or even anyone who had heard the story![26]

La Haye and Morris are so predisposed to believe

such secondhand hearsay that they seek to explain away Smith's on-the-spot evidence (or lack of it). They propose that since Resit was a Muslim (a fact that they do not verify), he would not have wanted to cooperate with the Christian ark-searchers, nor would any of the persons for miles around—despite the fact that Smith offered a reward for information. No concrete evidence for such local hostility is offered.

One must be even less charitable toward Balsiger and Sellier, who, thirty years later, still repeat the Resit story as valid evidence for the ark's survival, not even mentioning the fact of Smith's unsuccessful expedition.[27]

Summary and Conclusions

Research into this type of evidence for the ark's survival is, like that of the other areas, fraught with difficulties. (1) The sources are often third- and fourth-hand. Years could be and have been spent in trying to verify some of them. (2) The original documents often cannot be found—if in fact they ever existed. (3) Alleged eye-witnesses have died and thus cannot verify the reports attributed to them, or clarify critical details. (4) The reports are filled with discrepancies, some minor but others so substantial as to raise the question of credability. (5) A few are expressed in such strident, polemical tones as to destroy any claim of objectivity. (6) Without questioning the integrity of some reporters, it appears that details have been added as their observations were retold.

The extent to which these accounts have been

and will continue to be believed depends, in some measure, upon what the hearer is already predisposed to believe. To the investigator who is not convinced that the ark has survived on the mountain, that is, who seeks evidence for a decision rather than confirmation of an opinion, perhaps the most that can be said is this: Hearsay evidence, in the absence of tangible proof, cannot be convincing. While one might believe that a structure of some sort (or at least timbers) exists on the mountain, its nature and origin cannot be determined from these reports. Based upon this evidence alone, one can at least say that further investigation is merited, but that "harder" evidence is needed in order to reach a decision. To the possibility of such evidence we now turn.

5 Recent Photographic Evidence

AS THE OLD ADAGE HAS IT, "THE CAMERA doesn't lie." So if, as is often claimed, there are photographs available of a boat-like structure high on Agri Dagi, that should be convincing proof that Noah's ark has survived. Or should it? An examination of this evidence is now in order.

Photographs of an object alleged to be the ark were reportedly taken during World War I and World War II.[1] These have never been produced for evaluation. Several pictures, however, are available from more recent days.

1. George J. Greene, an American mining engineer, allegedly took a series of photos from a helicopter in 1952, showing an area on the northeastern flank of Agri Dagi. This is the area of the Ahora Gorge, where most of the other sightings have been reported. The photos were lost when Greene was murdered in British Guiana about ten years later. Nearly thirty persons who claim to have seen the pictures say that a boat was clearly visible, even its planking, and that it was projecting from beneath a glacier. Sketches of the object have been made, based upon the memory of those who saw the photos.[2]

2. Aerial photos of an area six thousand feet above sea level and twenty miles south of Agri Dagi,

taken in 1959 as part of the Geodetic Survey of Turkey, show an oval-shaped object which some observers said was roughly the size of the ark in Genesis. A follow-up investigation on the ground revealed a natural geological formation.[8]

3. A 35mm slide of terrain on the mountain was taken by the Archaeological Research Foundation (ARF, a group of ark-searchers) in 1966. When reviewed two years later, it was noticed that the picture contained a small curiously shaped object near the base of a cliff.[4] Although the photographer, Eryl Cummings, has been very careful to describe the object as unidentified, the photo has been widely publicized as possible evidence for the survival of the ark. In 1972, another group from the Institute for Creation Research, a small college in California known for its opposition to Darwin's theory of evolution, tried to locate the area shown in the photograph and thereby help identify the object. They "felt they had located the object" in the Ahora Gorge, but it turned out to be "a rock formation, very uniform in shape, giving a finished appearance. Erosion had carved it out of intermittent layers of basalt and volcanic tuft, giving a definite appearance of a catwalk along the top."[5] Rather than concluding that the mystery of the "unidentified object" had been solved, the ICR group decided that the object in the photo must lie elsewhere: "the 'object' has not yet been relocated."[6]

4. In 1973, a photo of Agri Dagi was taken by the Earth Resources Technology Satellite (ERTS) from an altitude of 450 miles.[7] Subsequently, a "mail room and supply clerk"[8] at the ERTS Center

in Sioux Falls, South Dakota, noticed a "peculiar rectangular shape, apparently foreign to the mountain." This was called to the attention of ark-searcher John Montgomery, who saw in it support for the claim that the ark survived atop the mountain.[9] Subsequently a press release was made in 1974 by a U.S. Senator whom Montgomery had contacted, and the matter has thereafter received wide publicity.[10]

Apparently, NASA analysts who have been contacted about this matter agree that an object the size of the ark (300 × 50 cubits, that is, 450' × 75' *if* a cubit is reckoned at around 18 inches[11]) would scarcely be detectible from 450 miles by the ERTS cameras, and if so, only as a single "dot."[12] This seems to have been acknowledged later even by Montgomery, who nonetheless hopes that *future* satellite photos will prove more helpful in the search.[13]

5. In either 1974 or 1975, the Holy Ground Mission Changing Center in Palestine, Texas, produced a photo which they claim shows planking on the sides of the ark. It reportedly was taken high on the mountain with a telephoto lens from a distance of two thousand feet.[14]

The photo has been criticized by some persons on the following grounds: (a) The "boat" seems to be strangely in-focus (individual "planking" lines are clearly visible), whereas its surroundings are not. A telephoto lens, at that range, should make the focus uniform. Thus some persons regard the photo as composite.[15] (b) "The CIA has analyzed the picture and labeled it as a very amateurish example of a retouched photograph."[16] My inquiry to the CIA as to whether they had indeed examined the photograph produced the following response: "We have looked into your inquiry and are not able to provide any pertinent information." On July 19, 1977, just to make sure that I understand the statement properly, I called the Office of the Assistant to the Director of Public Affairs (who had signed the letter) and was informed that their files contained no information on this matter.

CENTRAL INTELLIGENCE AGENCY

WASHINGTON, D. C. 20505

PUBLIC AFFAIRS   11 July 1977
Phone (703) 351-7676

Mr. Lloyd Bailey
Duke University
The Divinity School
Durham, N. C. 27706

Dear Mr. Bailey,

    This is in response to your letter of 29 June 1977 seeking confirmation that CIA had determined that a photograph allegedly showing a wooden structure high on Mt. Ararat was not authentic. We have looked into your inquiry and are not able to provide any pertinent information. I regret that we cannot be helpful.

                                        Sincerely,

                                        Herbert E. Hetu
                                        Assistant to the Director
                                        for Public Affairs

Evaluation and Conclusions

Until the questions surrounding the authenticity of the photo from the Texas center (no. 5) are cleared up by examination of the negative, it should not be used as evidence. In the ERTS photo (no. 4), the object is too large to be the ark; it likely is a natural formation. At best, photo number 3 by the ARF remains an "unidentified object"; far more likely is the conclusion that it is a natural formation. The object in the aerial photos of 1959 (no. 2) has already been confirmed as a natural formation. That leaves only the photos by Greene (no. 1), which do not survive for analysis. Hence no conclusions can be based upon them.

But we must raise the following questions concerning Greene's material: (a) Was it genuine, or upon close analysis would questions have arisen about it as they have about the Holy Ground photograph? (b) Why were the photos not convincing to some of the persons who saw them? Were there differing opinions about what was shown? In any case, Greene failed to arouse interest in an expedition to recover the object. (c) Are twenty-five-year-old memories of the photos unquestionably reliable? Is it possible that suggestability and ark-recovery enthusiasm have influenced the clarity with which the object is remembered to be a boat, with planking intact? To these questions, no answer is possible.

In sum: there is no existing photographic evidence of a boat-like structure on Agri Dagi—to say nothing of evidence for Noah's ark.

6 Up and Down the Mountain Wood from the Ark

A PIECE OF WOOD FROM THE ARK! TO ACTU-
ally see such a relic—perhaps even to own a splinter
of Noah's ark—may be the fond hope of amateur
ark-searchers. To the more professional, however,
the matter is a good deal more serious. The recovery
of wood from Mount Ararat has become a lifetime
ambition and adventure.

Before considering in detail the wood found in recent years on Agri Dagi, we should note that over
the centuries wood from several arks has been reported. Tradition has it that ark wood was found on
Jabal Judi in Arabia, Mount Baris in Armenia, and
on an unnamed height in Adiabene. Pieces of ark
wood have been displayed in recent times from
Jabal Judi in Gordyene, from Jabal Judi in Arabia,
and, of course, from Agri Dagi (see chap. 3).

It is the Agri Dagi wood that has become famous—featured in the movie *In Search of Noah's
Ark* and in most of the popular ark books. And
much wood has been discovered on Agri Dagi over
the last fifteen hundred years. To summarize briefly,
the following persons have reported finding wood on
that mountain: Dutch traveler Jans Struys in 1670;
English diplomat James Bryce in 1876; Russian explorer E. de Markoff in 1888; New Zealander, Hardwicke Knight in 1936; the Armenian Alim, who dis-

played a piece of the ark "which had been in his family for centuries."[1] Most important for our survey is the wood found by French Industrialist Fernand Navarra in 1955 and 1969.

This wood brought down from Agri Dagi has come from many locations on the mountain (leading the movie to suggest that the ark was broken by an earthquake into two widely separated pieces). Descriptions of the color have varied widely—red, brown, green, blue, black. It has been described as soft and soggy—and so hard that a bullet or dagger would not penetrate it. In any case, no piece of the wood before Navarra's find is available for scientific analysis, and therefore no conclusion can be based on any of these accounts. The full case for the survival of Noah's ark of Agri Dagi must, to date, depend on the age of the wood recovered by Fernand Navarra.

During his 1955 expedition, Navarra separated a hand-hewn beam about five feet long from a mass of timbers projecting from beneath a glacier at an elevation of about 13,500 feet.[2] Specimens of it were submitted for analysis at a number of institutions,[3] including the Forestry Institute of Madrid, Spain, which assigned it an age of about five thousand years. Those who believed that the biblical account of the flood was literally true—and that the flood occurred around 2450 B.C.[4]—seemingly had their beliefs confirmed. The ark not only had survived, but had at last been undeniably recovered. Radiocarbon analysis, however, did not support such an early date for the wood.

In 1969, Navarra returned to the mountain with

members of a group calling themselves the Search Foundation, and more beams were recovered.[5] Specimens of this wood were also submitted for analysis, and the results are just beginning to appear.

The Radiocarbon Method of Dating

Radiocarbon dating, developed after World War II by Dr. Willard F. Libby at the University of Chicago, determines the age of things that lived during the last 20,000 to 30,000 years by measuring the amount of carbon 14 they contain. Carbon 14 is an unstable (radioactive) heavy form of carbon with an atomic weight of 14 (normal stable carbon has an atomic weight of 12). The half-life of carbon 14, formerly thought to be 5568 years, has been revised to 5730 years by recent calculations. This means that an ounce of carbon 14 is reduced by decay to half an ounce in 5730 years, that half the remainder decays during the next 5730 years, leaving a quarter of an ounce, and so on.

Carbon 14 forms constantly in the earth's upper atmosphere, and then combines with oxygen to form a variety of carbon dioxide that mixes with the earth's atmosphere and enters all living things through plant photosynthesis. When a plant or animal dies, there is no further intake of carbon 14. That already present at death goes on disintegrating at a constant rate, so that the amount of carbon 14 remaining is proportional to the time elapsed since death. Based on the carbon 14 content of living matter today and the half-life (disintegration rate) of carbon 14, it is possible to calculate the age of an organic sample.

The actual laboratory procedure for radiocarbon dating involves burning the sample to reduce it to pure carbon and then measuring its radioactivity (rate of atomic disintegration) in a form of geiger counter. The measurement is expressed as the number of carbon 14 disintegrations per minute per gram of carbon. Contemporary living samples have a 15.3 for this value, it is 7.65 for samples 5730 years old, and it is 3.83 for samples twice that age. The actual sample is compared with these values to determine its age. The margin of error (expressed as "± x years") is no more than 10 per cent back to 1000 B.C. and 20 per cent to 3000 B.C.

Radiocarbon Analysis of the 1955 Specimens

Five laboratories have subjected Navarra's wood to radiocarbon (C^{14}) analysis, with the following results:

1. The National Physical Laboratory, Teddington, Middlesex, England, found the wood to be 1190±90 years old—resulting in a date of 760 A.D.[6] ("corrected" 5730 half-life date: 790–770 A.D.).[7]

2. The University of California at Los Angeles gave 1230±60 years—or 720 A.D.[8] ("uncorrected" 5568 half-life date).

3. The University of California at Riverside—1210±90 years or 740 A.D.[9] ("uncorrected" 5568 half-life date).

4. Teledyne Isotopes (formerly Isotopes, Inc.), Westwood, New Jersey, tested the wood. I have not been able to secure a published report of this test,

but have confirmed it by telephone with James Buckley of Teledyne. His memory was that the test results differed "by a couple of centuries" from those of the other labs.[10] This alleged divergence, along with the Geochron report, may have contributed to the statement that radiocarbon test results place the wood between 1300 and 1700 years of age—that is, around 300–700 A.D.[11]

5. Geochron Laboratories, Cambridge, Massachusetts, gives an age of 1690±120—resulting in A.D. 260. However, since the sample was "inadequate" (only one half the amount of wood needed to fill the smallest counter), this test result may be questioned.[12]

Statements sometimes appear that tests of Naverra's wood were conducted by two other laboratories. However, the reported University of Pennsylvania Radiocarbon Laboratory's test[13] appears to have been done on the wood recovered by Navarra in 1969. A University of California at San Diego (La Jolla) test was mistakenly reported in *Science News* (vol. 111, pp. 198-99).

Radiocarbon Analysis of the 1969 Specimens

Two institutions have reported thus far on the wood Navarra recovered fourteen years later. The University of Pennsylvania gives the age of this as 1320±50 years—dating it to 640 A.D. ± 50 years (as "corrected" and based upon 5730 half-life).[14] Geochron Laboratories gives 1350±95 years—A.D. 600. If converted to the 5730 half-life and "corrected," that result would be A.D. 640–620.[15]

What Does This Radiocarbon Analysis Show?

The challenge to their theories that these test results present is apparently ignored by some ark-searchers,[16] quickly dismissed by others[17]—and occasionally explained as the result of repairs to the ark![18] That Navarra would have had the back luck, on both his expeditions, to find only hypothetical repair timbers is apparently quite acceptable to many ark-searchers. Only occasionaly does one find a systematic objection to the limitations of radiocarbon analysis.[19]

One common objection is that the results of tests on Navarra's wood differ so widely that they must be dismissed—or more generally, that they indicate the unreliability of the method itself.[20] In response, it must be pointed out that of the four verified tests on the 1955 wood, three are in very close agreement. The maximum difference is only forty years (and with an expressed margin of error of $\pm$ 60 to $\pm$ 90 years).

The fifth analysis, by Teledyne, as well as that of Geochron, could well be accounted for in the following fashion. The radiocarbon analyses do not indicate the date of the entire beam found by Navarra, but only of the small pieces which Navarra removed and shipped to the various labs. Moreover, the labs usually will have removed a still smaller section (about ten annual rings)[21] for the actual analysis. Thus, dates from the various tests might differ by as much as the entire growth-age (diameter) of the beam which Navarra removed from the mountain—that is, by years, perhaps even centuries. Navarra's documents are very imprecise in this regard. He seems to have submitted a cross section of 13cm (about five inches), with annual rings varying in thickness from 2mm to 4mm, to the National Museum of Natural History in Paris.[22] Provided that the specimens submitted elsewhere were from the same cross-section (which is *not* stated to be the case), this alone would allow for a variation in results of around 32 to 65 years. This, when added to a possible 60 to 90-year margin of error, goes a long way toward bringing the Teledyne and Geochron results into line with the strong consensus.

One more fact may account for the Teledyne and Geochron results. Navarra cut the single beam which he recovered from the mountain into four (?)[23] pieces for easy removal. The whole beam diminishes radically in diameter (that is, in number of annual rings) from one end to the other. Thus, sections removed at random for radiocarbon analysis could differ in age by many years. Until we have precise details as to the special relationship of the various test specimens, objections to the divergence of the Teledyne and Geochron tests are pointless.

Navarra's wood, showing the positions of the three pieces if the beam were refitted—illustrating the radical reduction in diameter.

As to the 1969 results, which agree very well with each other, it is actually no suprise that they differ by about a hundred years from the results for the 1955 specimens. After all, we are dealing with two separate beams (trees?), and it is not even self-evident that they are from the same structure. In any case, the tests indicate the date at which the particular annual rings being tested grew, not the date at which the entire beam was placed in a structure.

In short, objections to the radiocarbon tests, if they are based on the Teledyne and Geochron divergences, cannot be taken seriously. On the contrary, there is an amazing agreement.

Another objection has been that the great heights at which the wood has so long remained (about 13,-500 feet) might have had an effect upon the accuracy of the test results. Exposed to a higher amount of cosmic radiation (because of less atmospheric shielding) and hence to a higher level of C^{14}, the wood might appear younger than it actually is.[24] However, in an unrelated test, pieces of wood from near sea level and from around 10,000 feet elevation, and both the same age as verified by count of annual rings, have contained the same amount of C^{14}. This means that altitude will have had no effect upon the accuracy of the Navarra wood test results.[25]

Another objection holds that Navarra's wood may have been subjected to contamination by water-soluable C^{14}, and that this may have contributed to a false radiocarbon reading.[26] However, the early test conducted at Teddington, where, apparently, no decontamination procedures were followed, agrees closely with that at UCLA where specific steps were taken to remove secondary materials—that is, to meet this very objection. Teddington gives 790–770 A.D.; UCLA 720 A.D.[27] Hence, C^{14} contamination has been minimal. In any case, stringent decontamination procedures are now standard prior to radiocarbon analysis.

Can We Depend on Radiocarbon Analysis?

Radiocarbon scientists generally explain the divergence of C^{14}-derived dates from absolute dates by the following major factors:[28]

1. The change in the production rate of C^{14} in the earth's atmosphere, which is caused by variations in cosmic ray intensity. These variations depend upon the interplanetary magnetic field, solar flares, supernova variations, etc.[29]

2. Changes in the C^{14} production rate which are caused by variations in the earth's magnetic field, ranging from 1.6 of its present value about 400 B.C. to .5 of its present value about 4000 B.C.[30]

3. Change in the C^{14} balance between the oceans and the atmosphere caused by changes in global climate.[31]

These and other lesser factors have been carefully studied and voluminous statistics compiled in order to allow compensation for them in radiocarbon age determinations.

For example, there is a latitudinal difference in the amount of C^{14} in the atmosphere, caused in part by the concentration of the oceans in the Southern Hemisphere. It is about 4 percent less at 42 degrees south than at 42 degrees north, since the greater expanse of ocean means greater absorption. Contemporaneous samples from the two hemispheres have indicated that the ones from the south will test out about forty years older than those from the north.[32]

The most reliable and wide-ranging correction for all these factors, now standard procedure in testing wood, is comparison of C^{14}-derived dates with dendro-dates (annular ring counts) of the same specimens. Dendrochronologists, working primarily with the annular rings of bristlecone pines, now have a reliable chronology stretching back about 7,500 years.[33] The results, roughly, are that for samples dated by annular ring count to 1000 B.C. and later, radiocarbon dates will be accurate within about 100 years; dating from about 2000 B.C., the adjustment is about 350 years; from 3000 B.C. it is about 600 years: from 5000 B.C. it is about 800 years.[34] For material from earlier periods (beyond the range of the dendrochronological check), the divergence probably would be greater.

As this applies to Navarra's wood, it is useless to point out that radiocarbon dates are sometimes in error by 800 years,[35] since the age-range to which that margin of error applies is far removed from that of the Navarra test results. Radiocarbon dates in the period A.D. 450–974, as checked by tree-ring samples, are accurate within 50 years. To make matters worse for the ark-searchers' position, radiocarbon dates during this period are about 50 years too *old*; Navarra's wood, when "corrected," is even *younger* than the tests indicate.

It is likewise to no avail to point out that archaeologists often make little use of radiocarbon tests for dating objects.[36] This is simply because the archaeologist, for strata within the historical period, needs

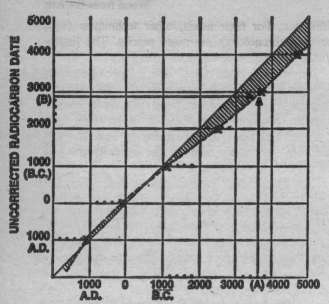

**RADIOCARBON DATE
AS "CORRECTED" BY TREE RINGS (DENDRO-DATE)**

Example: a specimen whose actual age, as determined by annular ring count (dendro-date), is 3600 B.C. (point A), will give a radiocarbon reading of about 2950 B.C. (point B), 650 years too young. However, for the period roughly 500 B.C. to A.D. 1300, the radiocarbon reading will be slightly too old, and it is within this range that Navarra's specimens fall.

(For greater detail, see *MASCA Newsletter,* IX August, 1973.)

dates that are accurate within a few decades—a century at most—and radiocarbon tests do not yield such precise results, especially for items older than

1000 B.C. For their needs, other techniques (e.g., ceramic chronology) are more precise. The limitation is fine precision, not gross error.[37]

The dendrochronological check on radiocarbon dating is not without its own problems, the main one being that some species of trees may, under certain climatic conditions such as late frost, produce more than one ring per year.[38] Fortunately, however, this has been "extremely rare" in the carefully checked history of bristlecone pines.[39]

In sum: while the radiocarbon method often produces results that are not precise enough for archaeologists working in regions with well-established chronologies, and while further refinements are necessary and possible, it is still the most reliable determination of age. For prehistoric archaeologists, it is often the only available method of dating.

Other Methods of Dating Navarra's Wood

Color and density change was used by the Forestry Institute in Madrid, Spain, which estimated the wood to be about five thousand years old. The color was black; the density 1.100. The species of tree was identified as a white oak (*Quercus pedunculata* Ehrh.), said to have an average density while living of .800–.850. Thus the change in density during its years atop the mountain would be approximately .275.[40]

The Department of Anthropology and Prehistoric Studies of the University of Bordeaux, France, dated the wood by degree of lignitization, which is an initial state in the formation of coal. This led to their opinion that the specimen dated to "a remote antiquity." The Madrid Forestry Institute's identification as *Quercus pedunculata* was specifically dismissed in favor of another species of white oak, *Quercus cerris* L., said to have an average density while growing of .925. Another oak, *Quercus castaneifolia* Mey., with a density of .938, was suggested as a second option.[41]

No method or criteria show up at all in the reported 4,500 years age[42] allegedly assigned to the wood by the Center for Forestry Research and Analysis, Paris, France. Their documents, as published by Navarra[43] make no mention even of date. They did identify the wood as *Quercus robur* L., again an oak.

Finally, an "expert" at the Cairo Museum, without conducting any scientific tests, is said to have assigned an age of 4,000–6,000 years.[44]

The movie *In Search of Noah's Ark* (see chap. 7) summarizes the methods which the producers feel are valid in dating Navarra's wood:[45] degree of lignite formation;[46] gain in wood density; cell modification;[47] and degree of fossilization (silicification?). The results of each type of test, it is said, agree that the age of the wood is about 5,000 years—placing it well back to the period of Noah and his ark.

How Accurate Are These Methods?

The extent to which fossilization of wood—and related degradation processes—takes place will depend on several environmental factors, including available moisture, contents of the moisture (amounts and kinds of minerals, pH level), aeration (exposure to wind), temperature, and sedimentary setting, including pressure applied and the extent to which oxygen is excluded.[48] It also depends on the length of time during which the environmental factors have been in effect.

For example, environments may differ so radically that some 12,000-year-old specimens may be more fossilized than others which are 12,000,000 years old.[49] Or the initial stages of siliceous fossilization may, under favorable conditions, be observed in as little as thirteen years.[50] Further, one must know not only the relationship of the various factors but also whether they have remained constant throughout the entire time that the wood was exposed to them. Thus, simple linear degradation formulas for computing the age of a wood specimen are not possible (such as: X-extent of fossilization, or related condition, indicates that Y-amount of time has passed).

Such a formula for dating Navarra's wood could be worked out only if (1) all the environmental factors that operate at the 13,500-foot elevation of Agri Dagi were known; (2) the history of the mountain were fully known, so that we could be certain that the environmental factors have remained constant or could know exactly when and to what extent they have changed—we know, for example, of two volcanic eruptions; (3) a control specimen were available—a piece of wood subjected to conditions similar to those on Agri Dagi and found to fossilize at such-and-such a rate.

Since none of these three conditions has been met, attempts to date Navarra's wood by the extent of fossilization and related conditions are totally meaningless.

As for the dark color of the wood, Dr. Francis Kukachka of the U.S. Forest Service, Wood Identification Bureau, Madison, Wisconsin, remarks: "The dark color and hardness of the wood is characteristic of white oak wood which has been exposed for a long period of time to water containing iron. The tannin in the wood reacts with the iron, producing the characteristic color and hardness and apparently makes the wood very resistant to natural degradation."[51] Kukachka is speaking of the 1969 wood, but I assume the same would apply to the 1955 specimen. In a phone call on November 4, 1977, Dr. Kukachka told me that he has seen specimens of white oak that had reached a dark color equal to that of Navarra's wood after having been immersed in water in a natural setting for no more than one hundred years. I assume, therefore, that change of color, as an alleged means of dating the wood, is worthless.

The change-in-density criterion for dating is subject not only to the limitations just discussed but to another as well. The species of the wood being examined must be determined beyond all question, since the average-density-while-growing is the basis of the computation. The widely quoted Madrid age—five thousand years—assumes that the species is *Quercus pedunculata* (average density .825, i.e., density change .275). But the Bordeaux report, seldom quoted in this regard, specifically rejects the Madrid identification and proposes instead *Quercus cerris* (average density .925, i.e., a density change of .175). Assuming a linear rate of degradation, this alone would seem to reduce the age of Navarra's wood to 3,200 years.[52] And the problem is even more severe. Since each individual tree of a species has an individual environment while growing, it is precarious to quote an "average density" for a species. Variations may be rather extreme—indeed, so much so that density range cannot be a reliable guide to species identification. Thus an age computation based upon density change, ignoring all the previous limitations, would be accurate only to the extent that the specimen, while growing, conformed to the assumed average density.

But is even this the end of the density change problem? According to the Madrid report,[53] the specimen submitted for analysis had two consistencies: a soft outer area and a hard inner core. The report, in translation, is ambiguous as to whether the present density of 1.100 applies to the whole piece of wood or only to the inner core. In either case, the apparent nonuniformity of the change in density poses problems for determining the age.

I have submitted the documents published in Navarra's book, plus a list of the four criteria on which the movie depends for dating, for evaluation to the Department of Wood and Paper Science of North Carolina State University's School of Forest Resources. The reply[54] included the following summary:

Degree of "lignitization," gain in wood density, cell modification, and degree of fossilization are most unreliable estimates of aging of naturally exposed wood. The exposure variables are so unknown, and so unpredictable, that to apply steady-state laboratory degradation formulas just is not credible for these purposes. Certainly color is the least precise criterion of aging that I could suppose. . . . I find it impossible to accept an age of 5000 years for the wood specimens in question, but I would accept a date in the early centuries of the Christian era.

Even ardent ark-searcher John Morris, speaking of these same four criteria, considers them to be "highly subjective and unreliable techniques . . . rather uncertain estimates . . . rejected by most scientists."[55]

Other Wood on Agri Dagi

Not only have pieces of wood been brought down from the heights of Agri Dagi, a considerable amount has been carried up it as well. Consider the following instances:

In 1829 Professor Friedrich Parrot carried up two heavy crosses, five feet and ten feet long, the latter made of beams six inches square. The larger cross was erected at the 16,000-foot level, and the smaller one on the summit.[56]

A wooden cross seven feet high and made of *oak* was erected high on the western slope by Hermann von Abich in 1845.[57]

The Russian Colonel J. Khodzko erected a seven-foot cross on the summit in 1859.[58]

A "small wooden container" was left at the summit in 1902 by the Russian expedition headed by Ivangouloff.[59]

In addition, we know that there were several larger structures on the mountain, all partially built of wood. These include the Monastery of St. James at 6,350 feet; the Chapel of St. Gregory at 8,300 feet; various huts in which Struys stayed during his ascent of the mountain;[60] a house attributed to Noah.[61]

Obviously, then, a great deal of wood has been carried up the mountain, and our records likely cover but a fraction of the total amount. Is it possible that such wood might be, or even has been, discovered by later expeditions and mistaken for part of the ark?

The Agri Dagi Wood—A Final Observation

From tests run so far, we can find no reliable indication that Navarra's wood is older than the eighth/seventh century A.D. Even ardent ark-searcher John Morris remarks (but based on other grounds): "The Navarra wood remains highly questionable in origin,[62] and Navarra's claim to have found the ark is at best premature."[63]

7 The Movie
IN SEARCH OF
NOAH'S ARK

WIDELY DISTRIBUTED TO LOCAL THEATERS and recently shown on network television,[1] this popular movie has provided an enjoyable adventure for its viewers, whether ark-enthusiasts or not. Certainly it has aroused wide interest in the search for the ark, and likely will make some converts to the group of ark-searchers.

The movie has the following major parts.[2] (1) A reenactment of the Genesis account of the flood, in rather literal terms. The Bible is seen as literal history, and the movie attempts to show how archaeology allegedly has verified it. Geographical and geological evidence for a worldwide flood is cited, as well as flood stories from the literature of other cultures. (2) A reenactment of ancient and recent attempts to recover the remains of the ark. The basic assumption is that all the attempts were made on Agri Dagi and that it is the only possible landing-site. (3) Discussion of the ark's size, contents, sea-worthiness, etc., including interviews with several persons who supply technical information to support the literal truth of the ark story. (4) A review of the various photographs which have been claimed to show the remains of the ark on Agri Dagi. (5) A review of various tests conducted on the wood recovered by Navarra. (6) An analysis of satellite photos of the Agri Dagi area.

This book, in keeping with the boundaries for discussion laid out in chapter 1, will not discuss such wider problems as whether the biblical account of the flood should be understood literally or even whether such a worldwide flood is geographically or geologically possible. However, in the light of the matters that we have examined in the previous chapters, other claims made in the movie can be evaluated. For example, *In Search of Noah's Ark* should *not* have suggested or claimed:

1. That Sir Leonard Woolley, when he excavated the site of ancient Ur, Abraham's hometown, found evidence of a flood which supports the biblical account. On the contrary, anyone can discover, by reading Woolley's report,[8] that the "flood" at Ur did not even destroy the entirety of that city, to say nothing of the entire world. The movie has repeated an old claim that has by now been widely renounced. *but geological strata knewbwthe*

2. That "*all* indications seem to point to a universal deluge." Archaeologically, at least, there is *no* evidence of such an event,[4] and many experts in the fields of geology, geography, and comparative literature would deny that such evidence is to be found in their areas as well. Such sweeping over-statements are often found in the movie. It has a fondness for citing "the scientific community," "scholars," and "scientists," as if there were strong, if not near-unanimous, support for the movie's claims among such groups. This is simply not in accordance with the facts.

83

3. That ancient attempts to reach the remains of the ark were ended after a number of accidents. No evidence is offered for this statement, and to my knowledge there is none. (See chap. 3, section 5.)

4. That there is evidence, "as early as 300 B.C.,"[5] presumably from Berossus, that the ark came to rest upon and survived upon "Mount Ararat"—meaning Agri Dagi. Not only is that unlikely, but also no mention should have been made of Nicolas of Damascus or of Josephus in support of this location (see chap. 3).

5. That there is a city in the vicinity of Mount Ararat whose ancient name means "the place of first descent" (see chap. 3 and Appendix I).

6. That Robert ("Believe It or Not") Ripley, who "has never been proved wrong," found the remains of the Tower of Babel at Borsippa in Mesopotamia and "what natives believe to be" the tomb of Noah in the mountains of Lebanon. Actually, the massive ruins at Borsippa (Birs Nimrud) are several miles removed from what is now known to be ancient Babylon (Babel) where the tower was built. Even a source as "conservative" as Henry Halley's *Pocket Bible Handbook*[6] suggests that the traditional nineteenth-century location at Borsippa should be given up. And, for the sake of consistency, the movie ought to have honored the Armenian claim that the tomb of Noah is to be found near Agri Dagi rather than far away in the mountains of Lebanon. And note that Ripley is not quoted as having located Noah's tomb, but only as having found a tradition about its location. Clearly, he is not likely to be "proved wrong" about that.

But exactly what the *movie* was trying to prove by such cleverly worded material is far from clear to me.

7. That explorer James Bryce found wood at the 14,000-foot level of Agri Dagi, and thus near other "finds." However, Bryce's own account puts it at about 13,000 feet. In addition, the movie seems far more confident that a part of the ark had been found than Bryce himself actually was (see chap. 4).

8. That contamination and a changing environment atop the mountain, which allegedly would make radiocarbon dates for Navarra's wood unreliable, may be ignored when other test methods are applied. That is, having brushed aside the radiocarbon results in a sentence or two, the movie asks what reliable methods are available and then suggests extent of fossilization, gain in density, etc. In actuality, those methods are even less reliable, and for the very reasons that radiocarbon analysis was condemned (see chap. 6).

9. That an ERTS satellite "photographed Noah's ark." Even enthusiastic ark-searchers have found that claim impossible to accept (see chap. 5 and below).

10. That the Cummings photo ("unidentified object") and the Holy Ground Mission Changing Center photo are valid evidence, without mentioning the substantial doubts that have been raised about them even among major ark-searchers (see chap. 5). Moreover, the language of the movie often has a subtleness that might escape the notice of some casual viewers. For example, "*If* the broken ark

85

theory is valid, this [the Cummings photo] *would be* the lower half . . .".

11. That widespread doubt about the existence of the ark atop Agri Dagi springs from modernistic anti-biblicism and lack of faith. On the contrary, most of the doubts have arisen because of the weakness of the evidence and because of ark-searchers' misuse of sources—neither of which the movie bothered to point out to its viewers.

12. That radiocarbon dates for Navarra's wood range from 1,300 years to 2,100 years of age (that is, from 150 B.C. to A.D. 650). While I will not deny that this is true, my own survey of the various labs has led to a quite different range of results: A.D. 260 to 790 (see chap. 6).

In addition, there are three interesting aspects of the movie to be noted.

1. While the narrator was discussing the various laboratory reports (other than radiocarbon) on the age of Navarra's wood, he held in his hand a thick collection of documents, likely totaling several hundred pages. However, the reports, as published in Navarra's book, with no indication that they are shortened versions, total perhaps a dozen pages only.

2. Some of the nonradiocarbon tests were said to indicate an age for the wood of 4,484 years. However, Navarra's book indicates that this was a radiocarbon test result. In any case, that a laboratory test, radiocarbon or otherwise, would assign such a precise date seems unlikely. Even other ark-searchers have wondered if such a test result was not "con-

trived with a preconceived date [for the flood] in mind."[7]

3. Some viewers will have noted with interest, and perhaps humor, the way in which the testimony of the Babylonian priest Berossus is presented. While he would have written in Greek, basing himself upon earlier Akkadian (cuneiform) accounts, the movie shows us an Egyptian (heiroglyphic) text as background while the narrator discusses his account. There are not, to my knowledge, any Egyptian heiroglyphic accounts of the ark's survival. Does this indicate that the writers and producers of the movie do not know one language from another?

The most impressive part of the movie, and the one apparently containing new data, concerns a computerized examination of the intensity with which various parts of the mountain reflect sunlight. The claim is made that an area of the ERTS photo (see chap. 5), near the snow line where Navarra's wood was supposedly found ("where the ark is believed to be located"), has a reflective pattern that exists nowhere else on the mountain.[8] However, the following problems must be resolved before one can conclude, as does the movie, that this unique light pattern indicates that Noah's ark—or any foreign object—lies there.

(a) Would the area retain its unique reflectivity under different light conditions as alleged (that is, if the sun shone upon it at a different angle or intensity)? Would other areas on the mountain then display unique reflectivity? Only analysis of other photos can answer such questions.

(b) Why did the village of Ahora, and especially its reported tin roof,[9] not display unique reflectivity?

(c) Since an object the size of the ark is admittedly beyond the capacity of the ERTS cameras to capture on film (see chap. 5), as even ark-searchers admit, how can this pattern of unique reflectivity possibly be the ark?

(d) The nature of an object that displays unique reflectivity cannot be determined merely by noticing the fact that it does reflect light in a curious way. That is, we cannot automatically conclude that the object is foreign to the mountain or that it is wood, whether ancient or modern. Rather, all one can say is that, based on one photo taken at a given time and angle, there is an object of unknown identity, which, at that moment, reflected light in a unique way.

Nonetheless, this intriguing phenomenon calls for further investigation, and it may support the near certainty that a structure of some sort (though not necessarily a boat) lies beneath the edge of the snow on Agri Dagi (see chap. 8).

8 The Mystery of "Mount Ararat"

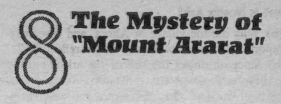

WHERE HAVE OUR INVESTIGATIONS LED THUS far? Are the remains of Noah's ark still hidden beneath the snows of "Mount Ararat"—Agri Dagi—in modern Turkey? If not, what is there on the mountain that excites present-day ark-searchers?

We have examined the accounts of the ancient witnesses—and found there are none prior to the eleventh/twelfth century A.D. (chap. 3). Unquestionably genuine photographs of a boat-shaped object that is not a natural rock formation—if any ever existed—are not available at present (chap. 5). Eye-witness reports have turned out to be unreliable, since they contradict each other in major details (chap. 4). That leaves the question of the wood which has been brought down from the mountain, reportedly dating from the time of the biblical flood (chap. 6).

Whatever its origin, the twelve-hundred-year-old wood that Navarra recovered is a significant archaeological find, and it deserves further investigation in order to determine more precisely when, by whom, and why it was placed in such an unlikely spot. Further expeditions have been planned by several groups, but thus far the Turkish government has forbidden them to journey to the mountain.[1]

The mystery surrounding the wood is, at first

glance, deepened by the geography of the mountain itself. At times, it can be one of the least hospitable places on the surface of the earth. At the lower levels, there are dangerous predators—bears, wild dogs, wolves—and an abundance of poisonous snakes. At the upper levels, lack of oxygen can leave one gasping for breath or even incapacitated. There are hidden crevasses above the snow line as much as a hundred feet deep; temperatures as low as 40 degrees below zero; wind with velocities up to 150 miles per hour; avalanches of snow and stone that can be triggered by no more than a normal human voice; swirling mists almost daily; extremely unstable footing caused by loose rock debris; terrifying bursts of lightning; very little water.[2] It is easy to see why the tradition developed that it was impossible to reach the summit[3] or why Parrot's claim to have done so in 1829 was greeted with skepticism.[4] It is hardly surprising, then, that some modern persons have found it easier to believe that Navarra's wood is part of a boat that floated to the heights of the mountain during the Genesis flood than that it is part of some other structure that was carried up the mountain, timber by timber, in more recent times.

However, the harshness of the mountain is occasionally broken. During one brief season of the year, warm winds blow up from the surrounding plains and cause balmy weather to the line of perpetual snow (about 13,500–14,000 feet).[5] Bryce found night temperatures at the 12,000-foot level to be no less than 40 degrees F., and was able to climb to the top clad only in a light coat.[6] Lynch's Kurdish porters slept unprotected on the open ground at the 12,000-foot level, and he found the temperature at the summit to be around 20 degrees F.[7]

Thus, while on the one hand, determined adults have been defeated or killed by the mountain, on the other hand, Navarra's eleven-year-old son climbed to the snow line in 1955,[8] and Montgomery's son, also eleven, almost reached the summit in 1970.[9] Armenian Georgie Hagopian has related that at the age of ten, he and the necessary supplies were carried by his uncle "for the roughest part of the ascent."[10] Various persons have been able to carry heavy wooden crosses beyond the snow line and even to the summit (see chap. 6). Parrot was able to lead horses and oxen, laden with food and firewood to the 13,000-foot level.[11] There is nothing physically improbable, then, in the proposal that persons may have carried or hauled heavy timbers to the snow line and used them to build some sort of structure. And it is useful to remember that other structures have been erected on the mountain, although at lower altitudes (see chap. 6).

It has been said that the species of wood that Navarra recovered does not grow "within 300 miles of the mountain,"[12] or that the timbers were found "150 miles from the nearest tree."[13] (The latter statement likely means: 150 miles from a tree of the same species, since trees of various sorts are found nearby, for example on the adjoining Little Ararat.) This alleged distance is seen by some persons as proof that the structure, or "boat," was built elsewhere, possibly in Mesopotamia, and was carried by the waters of the flood to the top of the mountain.

However, the following evidence argues against that conclusion.

1. The species of Navarra's wood is far from clear. It has been variously identified by wood scientists as one of the following white oaks: *Quercus robur, Quercus pedunculata, Quercus cerris,* and *Quercus castaneifolia* (see chap. 6). The problem is caused by the fact that some species of white oak are difficult, if not impossible, to differentiate in a deteriorated condition. Therefore, it seems questionable, if not impossible, to assert that *the* species of Navarra's wood does not grow within a certain distance of the mountain.

2. Even *if* the wood grew only at a distance from the mountain, there is nothing improbable in the suggestion that the timbers were brought there *overland*. The Assyrians, Babylonians, and Egyptians, for example, regularly bought massive cedar trees in the mountains of Lebanon and transported them hundreds of miles, by land and water, for use in their own lands.[14]

3. In fact, *all* the species suggested for Navarra's wood (above), rather than growing only at a great distance from the mountain, seem to grow nearby. Even Balsiger and Sellier[15] quote testimony that white oaks grow "abundantly in the peri-Mediterranean region" and make no mention of any alleged distance between Agri Dagi and where the wood must have grown. *Encyclopaedia Britannica* gives the following information: *Q. robur* "is a native of most of the milder parts of Europe and of the Caucasus Mountains of Asia"; *Q. cerris,* "the Turkey oak . . . abounds all over the Turkish peninsula, on

92

the Taurus ranges, and in many parts of southern Europe."[16] More detailed information comes from Edmond Boissier's standard reference work: *"Q. pedunculata* is found in Anatolia, Cappadocia, Turkish Armenia in the Province of Musch (just north of Lake Van, and adjoining Airarat); *Q. robur* in the Armenian Province of Musch; *Q. cerris* in the Amanus Mountains and in northern Anatolia; *Q. castaneaefolia* in the Transcaucasian Province of Talysch."[17]

It would be precarious for even an expert on the trees of northeastern Turkey to state emphatically that such-and-such a species does not grow within a specific distance of Agri Dagi. Certainty would require an on-the-spot examination of every square mile of territory within that distance. It is doubtful that such surveys have ever been made for the area, and in any case I have not found evidence that an expert has voiced an opinion about the range of the species of Navarra's wood. How much more skeptical ought one to be, therefore, concerning off-the-cuff remarks about this matter by American-born ark-searchers who may qualify as little more than tourists to the area of Agri Dagi.

4. Even *if* none of the species mentioned above now grows within some distance of the mountain, there is no reason to think that this was always the case. We know, for example, that depletion of forests in the ancient Near East began as early as 2500 B.C. and was especially pronounced in the last century.[18] In the case of Agri Dagi, we have specific testimony from medieval Arab geographers that, during their time, it was heavily forested. For exam-

ple, al-Istakhri mentions that nearby villagers cut firewood on its slopes, and al-Mukaddasi (al-Makdisi) says that more than a thousand villages were located on its flanks.[19] Both wrote during the tenth century A.D.

There is no need, therefore, to propose that the timbers which Navarra found have been transported any distance—either by land or by flood waters. They may have been fashioned from trees felled on the lower elevations of Agri Dagi.

To return to that mysterious structure. What might it have been, if not Noah's ark? Until there is further investigation, certainty in this matter is impossible. In the meanwhile, several plausible conjectures have been, or may be, offered.

1. A chapel,[20] perhaps to commemorate the ark's supposed landing site. We know definitely of two religious structures further down the mountain—the Monastery of St. James (Jacob), located at 6,350 feet and named for the Bishop of Nisibis who sought the ark on Ararat (see chap. 3), and the Chapel of St. Gregory, situated at 8,300 feet and named for the monk who brought Christianity to Armenia. They seem to have been founded around the ninth to the eleventh century,[21] and they were destroyed in the earthquake of 1840. While an additional chapel at the 13,000 to 14,000-foot snow line, where Navarra found his wood, would be more difficult to build, it is well to remember that the Byzantines, at roughly the same time, were erecting chapels at far more difficult spots—for example, on the jagged rock peaks of islands in the Aegean Sea.

2. A replica of the ark, constructed some time af-

ter Agri Dagi came to be regarded by the local population as the landing place. "The industrious monks of the monastery, wishing to further their own livelihood by the tourist trade, may have built something up on the mountain that with great difficulty could be seen and shown to be the 'Ark' "—so wrote the respected American archaeologist, G. Ernest Wright.[22] This explanation would seem to rely upon the hearsay eye-witness accounts that there is a *boat-shaped* structure on the mountain (see chap. 5).

Noorbergen, believing that a replica would be mentioned in Armenian records, has searched various archives, including the Jerusalem Armenian Convent. No such evidence was found.[23] In my view, such an absence of literary evidence proves nothing. Had such a replica been constructed, the monks would have tried to avoid any record of their activity.

3. A replica of the house which, says tradition, Noah built on the mountain after disembarking from the ark. The French Dominican Jordanus reports, in the fourteenth century: "In a certain part of the mountain is a dwelling which Noah is said to have built on leaving the ark."[24] But since he goes on to talk of the vine which Noah planted, placed by tradition near the village of Ahora on the lower elevations of the mountain, it is not at all clear that he understood the "house" to be near the snow line.

4. A hut for the use of hermits or climbers on the mountain. Several of these are reported by the Dutchman Jans Struys in the seventeenth century (Montgomery, *Quest*, pp. 102–3).

95

5. Timbers carried up the mountain by recent ark searchers (see above, chap. 6).

The second and third suggestions about the origin and purpose of the wood, if not the first as well, presuppose that Agri Dagi had already come to be regarded by the local population as the landing site of Noah's ark. But, as we have seen (chap. 3), there is no literary evidence for such an opinion prior to the eleventh century A.D., whereas Navarra's wood seems to come from the seventh/eighth century (see chap. 6). Might this indicate that the timbers were, after all, not connected with the ark story, but rather were part of some unknown structure from an earlier period, as in suggestion four?

However, we must remember that the radiocarbon tests indicate only the date of growth of the particular annular rings being tested. They do not indicate how much longer a tree continued to grow—that is, the date at which it was felled for timber or at which it died a natural death. Even less so do they indicate when a piece of timber would later have been used or even reused in erecting a building of some sort. More specifically, the timber found by Navarra in 1955 represents a tree that has been hewn until, apparently, only heartwood remained. The specimen received for analysis by the National Center of Scientific Research had a cross-section (diameter across the grain) of 13 cm—about 5.2 inches.[25] The University of Bordeaux *estimated* that the total heartwood of the tree, before it was hewn, had a diameter of *at least* 50 cm—about 20 inches.[26] Since, according to the National Center analysis, the annular rings had a thickness of 2-4 mm each, the age of the heartwood section alone would be a minimum of eighty-three years.[27]

But, what would be the diameter of sapwood which surrounded these eighty-three years of growth reflected in the heartwood have been? That is, what was the total age of the tree? Precision in this matter is impossible, since there are so many unknown variables—exact species, soil conditions, nature of growing seasons, etc. However, Balsiger and Sellier, *presumably* after having consulted competent resource persons about the matter, report that "Navarra's sample came from a tree about five feet in diameter with a height of about 150 feet."[28] *If so,* then the total age of the tree would be about 250 years.[29]

If the radiocarbon tests were conducted from specimens at the center of the heartwood, then (using the Teddington test results as an illustration, see chap. 6) the tree began to grow about the year 780 A.D. ±90. Adding 254 years, it would have been felled about the year 1034 A.D. ±90. Only after that date could the structure on the mountain have been erected. This early eleventh century date would seem to agree very well with other relevant data: (a) the two chapels erected lower down on the mountain about the eleventh century; (b) the earliest literary evidence that Agri Dagi was regarded as the ark's landing place only after the eleventh/twelfth century.

It is curious that the wood was found precisely at the elevation that marks the upper limit possible for construction. It is thus at the precise height, and from the exact time period, which we would expect for an ark replica, Noah's house replica, or chapel on the mountain. And since the perpetual snow line fluctuates slightly from season to season, depending upon the intensity of the previous summers and winters, it is not unlikely that a structure erected just beneath the line would later become encased in ice and snow.

In conclusion, have we solved the mystery of Noah's ark on Ararat? Almost certainly not to the satisfaction of all ark-searchers and other interested persons, but at least a reasonable solution has been proposed. Only further on-the-spot investigation will solve the matter. In the meanwhile, it is hoped that these chapters will have made a constructive contribution to the debate.

Appendix I

Heinrich Hübschmann, "Armeniaca," in Strass-
burger Festschrift zur XLVI Versammlung
Deutscher Philologen und Schulmänner
(Strassburg: Verlag von Karl Taübner, 1901),
pp. 69–79. [section 5, pp. 73–79, trans. Ben
and Beth Weisbrod, candidates for the M.
Div. degree at Duke University.]

5. Arm. Naxčavan: ἀποβατήριον?

In his admirable volume, Ararat und Masis (Hei-
delberg, 1901), F. Murad has attempted to present
evidence for a native Armenian flood story, the
scene of which is said to have been the majestic
Mount Masis[1] located in the Province of Airarat,
and which supposedly gave rise to the designation
Naxčavan[2] for a city lying approximately one
hundred kilometers southeast of the mountain
(Murad, p. 62). The city, which lay in the Province
of Vaspurakan according to the Geography attributed to Moses of Chorene, was later attributed to the
Province of Siunikh, and according to Armenian tradition was the residence of Noah after the landing of
the ark. Hence the residence came to be called
Naxčavan (= Naxijavan), which means "first set-

99

tling place" (from *nax*, "at first, before, prime," and *iǰawan*, "shelter, temporary quarters, station, stopping place"; p. 63).[8]

Thus when Josephus (*Antiq*. 1.92) says of the place where the ark landed: ἀποβατήριον μέντοι τὸν τόπον τοῦτον Ἀρμένιοι Καλοῦσιν. ἐκεῖ γὰρ ἀνασωθείσης τῆς λάρνακος ἔτι νῦν οἱ ἐπιχώριοι τὰ λείψανα ἐπιδεικνύονσι "[the Armenians call this place 'the Place of Descent' [Ἀποβατήριον] for it was there that the ark came safely to rest, and they show relics of it to this day"], it is natural for one to see therein verification for that [Murad's] explanation of the [Armenian] name and at the same time evidence for the antiquity of the Armenian flood tradition.

By capably dismissing opposing arguments, Murad appears to furnish evidence for his position. While I agree with him on almost all the details, I cannot agree with his central thesis for the following reasons.

1. *The etymology*. Murad's explanation of the name would be correct if the original form of the name were Naxiǰavan or Naxiǰevan, since: (a) the adverb *nax* (in contrast to *apa*, "thereupon, next, then, afterward") means "beforehand, first of all," and in compound forms it means "before, in advance, previously," or "ahead (Latin: *prae-*), first" [for example, *nax-at'or* means "front seat"; *naxotǰoin* means "the first to be greeted"; *nax-a-gah*, "chairmanship, precedence over someone"; *nax-a-stełc*, "first created" (Adam); *nax-cin*, "firstborn"; *nax-asaçeal*, "prophesied, predicted"; *nax-a-xnamut'iun*, "providence"; *nax-imaçut'iun*, "to know beforehand"; etc. (pp. 65-66)], and since (b) *iǰawan* (= ·iǰawank‘) means "temporary quar-

ters, shelter" (so also, *iǰavan, iǰevan,* from *ēǰ, ēǰ-kʻ,*
"dismount, descend," plus *wan-kʻ,* "shelter-dwell-
ing"; cf. *autʻe-wankʻ,* "quarters for the night"). Thus,
in Old Armenian, Naxiǰawan or Naxiǰavan would
mean "previous temporary quarters, previous shelter, first shelter," and could be so named in contrast
to the later stations passed through by the descendants of Noah in their further migration and expan-
sion.

But, an Old Armenian Naxiǰavan is not attested.
Instead, one finds Naxčavan or Naxčuan (and in
Murad's view, Naxǰavan), which, in current opinion, "is an abbreviation of Naxiǰavan that resulted
from the rapid pace of popular speech" (p. 63). At
present, however, abbreviations of this kind have
not been demonstrated in Old Armenian, and they
are not evident as far as I can see. *Iǰavan* (which
probably originated from *ēǰavan*[4] according to Armenian rules) would have to retain the *i* in compound with *nax,* just as it retains the *i* in *naximač,*
etc. The *i* or *u* which begin words of two or more
syllables also are not dropped in the formation of
compounds. Murad's explanation of this word, although otherwise correct, fails in light of this rule.

Furthermore, the forms Naxiǰavan, Naxiǰevan,
Naxǰavan, [and] Naxǰuan (along with Naxčavan
and Naxčuan), are traceable in documents only after the tenth century (p. 103), whereas for earlier
times the current form is Naxčavan or less frequently Naxčuan. For example, see Faustus, p. 173;
Lazar Pharpetsi, p. 369; Moses of Chorene, pp. 77,
129, 219 (Naxǰavan only at p. 57); Moses' *Geography,* p. 609 (Naxčuan); Sebeos frequently (see

Murad, p. 103; also in the Petersburgh ed., 1879, pp. 92, 93, 94, 118, 150); Levond (Petersburgh, 1887, p. 24 (according to the manuscript), p. 33 (instead of the Naxiǰevan of the Paris Press edition of 1857); Stephanos of Taron (Petersburgh, 1885), pp. 115, 120, 124 (instead of the Naxčivan of the Paris ed. of 1859); Thomas Artsruni (Petersburgh, 1887), pp. 78, 92, 105, 128, 195, etc. Thus, in the tenth century, only Joh. Katholikos (Murad, p. 103) frequently uses Naxǰavan,[5] and Moses Kalankatuatsi in his third book uses Naxiǰevan twice.[6] In any case, Naxǰavan, and even more so Naxiǰevan, is a later form of the name which originated with copyists of late manuscripts of the historians and with modern editors of the older texts.

If, however, Naxčavan is the earliest form of the name,[7] it obviously cannot be explained as "the first settling place" (nax-iǰavan). Rather, it becomes an otherwise unknown Naxč- (from Naxič- or Naxuč-), which was perhaps a name, plus (the well-known) *avan*, "market-town, country-town" (between the size of a village and a city),[8] and thus means: Naxič- or Naxuč-market-town. This may be compared with such place-names as Anušavan, Aršakavan, Bagavan (Baguan), Zarehavan (Zarehuan), Thornavan, Karčavan, Širakavan, Vataršavan, and Smbatavan.

2. *The [flood] tradition.* F. Murad (p. 67) must acknowledge [the correctness of] the statements of L. Alischan and Gelzer that the Old Armenian authors "up to the eleventh or twelfth century never speak of Mount Masis as the landing place of the ark; rather, when they mention the mountain [of the

ark] at all, they designate it as the Qardu Range."
However, he will not conclude (in contrast to them)
that the oldest [native Armenian] tradition did not
recognize Mount Masis as the mountain of the ark.
Rather, he sees evidence in the words of Johannes
Erznkatsi (ca. 1250–1326) that the connection between the flood story and Mount Maṣis had been a
generally recognized fact from time immemorial:
"the Ayrarat-mountain, the high-topped Mount
Masis, since it became the resting place of the ark"
(Murad, p. 69). [But] that is an unqualified exag-
geration of the evidence offered by Johannes
Erznkatsi, for it only proves that at his time Mount
Masis was generally considered to be the mountain
of the ark—not that it had always been considered
so. As to the question of the age of this [flood] tradition, we can only rely upon the evidence of the
older texts—which regardless of translation or original—do not connect the flood story with Mount
Masis.

The evidence, in which we find the same two versions of the flood story as in the older Jewish,
Greek, and Syrian authors (i.e., the Babylonian version in which the ark landed in the land of Qardu-
Gordyene, and the biblical version in which it
landed "on the mountains of Ararat," Gen. 8:4), is
as follows (Murad, pp. 26, 36 ff):

1. Eusebius [third century,] *Chronicle* (ed.
Aucher), vol. 1, pp. 36-37: "And of the ship (of
Xisuthros [= the Babylonian Ziusudra]) which
landed in Armenia, a small part still remains in the
Gordian (Arm.: Korduaçiḱ') Mountains (range)."

2. Faustus of Byzantium [fifth century] (Venice

ed. 1832), p. 22: "During that time, the great Bishop of Nisibis, the Holy Jacob, . . . left his city to journey to Mount Sararad[9] in the Armenian Mountains in the region of Airaratic control (domain)[10] in the Canton of Gordukh. . . . And he asked God to let him see the preserved ark that Noah had built which had come to rest on this mountain at the time of the deluge." *Saint*

3. The story of the Holy Hriphsime and her Companions (Moses of Chorene [eighth century?], *Opera*, Venice, 1865), p. 300: The Syrians say of Mount Soloph in Gordukh that "with the receeding of the flood waters, the ark arrived on the peak of the mountain, i.e., of Sararad (*i glux lerinn or ĕ Sararaday*), and that the sawfish halted the ship by passing through it; the place came to be named Themnis,[11] which means: 'eight souls got off the ark' " (see Murad, pp. 28-29; and cf. I Peter 3:20).

4. Thomas Artsruni [early tenth century] (Petersburgh, 1887), p. 19: "After the completion of the divine command, the ark was carried east by the waves to the middle of the world (*yareveleain? i miĵoç ašxarhi*) and rested on the mountains of Gordukh (*i lerins Korduaç*)." *East*

5. The Armenian translation [fifth century] of Genesis 8:4: "And the ark came to rest on the mountains of Ararat" (*i lerins Araratay*,[12] variant *Araraday*, for the Greek ἐπὶ τὰ ὄρη τὰ ᾿Αραράτ ["upon the mountains of Ararat"]).

If all these attestations stem directly or indirectly from Greek or Syrian sources (as in Murad's opinion), then the question arises as to whether there was a native Armenian flood story.

The only remaining passage in which the flood is mentioned is Moses of Chorene, *History*, vol. 1, chap. 6, p. 17. He reports from his informants Gorgi, Banan, and Davith (?) that one of these three took part in a Greek-style conversation about the distribution of peoples, and that the cleverest among them, Olompiodoros, had talked about names. He said,

I want to tell you unwritten stories which have come to us through tradition and which many peasants still tell to this day. There was a book about Xisuthros [Ziusudra] and his sons, which has not survived to the present, in which they say that the following portrayal is found: After Khsisuthros had floated to Armenia and had landed, one of his sons, named Sim, moved northwest to explore the land. He arrived at a small plain at the foot of an extensive mountain through which rivers flowed to the region of Assyria, lived on the river for two months, and named the mountain "Sim" after himself.[13] Then he returned to the southeast in the direction from which he had come. But one of the younger sons separated, with thirty sons and fifteen daughters and their husbands, from their father [Sim?] and took his dwelling place again on the same river bank,[14] after whose name (Tarban) he (Sim) also named the Canton of Tarôn. But he [Sim?] named the place where he lived "Cronk" ("Dispersion"), because the separation of his sons from him first began at that place. He [Sim?] turned away and lived, so they say, for some time on the borders of the region of Bactria, and one of his sons remained there. [The peope of] the Eastern Lands call the Sem [sic] "Zrvan," and the canton they call "Zaruand" to this day. Often the old peoples from the descendants of Aram relate this matter with loud music, song, and dance.

Where is Noah's Ark?

In this account, the names Xisuthros and Sim (= Sem), the equating of Sem with Zrvan, the explanation of Tarôn from Tarbon, of Zarvand from Zrvan, and the entire intent, are not accounted for by popular Armenian tradition but rather prove the learned workmanship of Moses. Also, the assertion that the descendants of Aram mention these matters is, in view of the notorious unreliability of Moses, too ambiguous for conclusions to be drawn from it. Even if this account had a popular basis, which I deny, then the scene of the story would be west and south of Lake Van, and the landing place of Xisuthros, according to the location of Mount Sim (see Moses, p. 80; Aristakes, *Last.*, p. 94) and the above account, would not be Mount Masis in [the Province of] Airarat, but in the land of Gordukh!

Thus Armenian literature of the fifth through the tenth centuries knows nothing of Masis as the mountain of the ark. When that identification is made at a later time, it is sufficiently explained as the result of the increasing influence of the Bible, which puts the landing place in the mountains of Ararat (= Arm. Airarat). Since the highest and most famous of these mountains was Masis, [it would be thought that] the ark must have landed there.[15] Since, at the same time, the Old Armenian Naxčavan came to be called Naxijevan, which was explained as the "first temporary lodging," it was natural to connect this city with the misplaced landing of the ark on Masis, so that legend and etymology now supported each other.

Be that as it may, there is no trace of a native [Armenian] flood story and no possibility of an ex-

planation of Naxčavan (or even of Naxjavan) as
ʼΑποβατήριον.[16] Josephus merely leaves us with his
statement that the ark's location was "in Armenia,
on the peak of a mountain," and speaks neither of
the Province ʼΑραράτ nor of the mountain Masis nor
of the city Ναξυάνα. His assertion that the Armenians named a place ʼΑποβατήριον in connection with
the flood story cannot be considered reliable. He
does not name his source, and we have no grounds
for accepting it forthwith even if it were Armenian.
Even an Armenian could have given him a false account of an Armenian place-name, and such would
be the case if he had explained Naxčavan to him
[Josephus] as the landing place.

Appendix II

The following evaluation of Faustus' account (see chap. 3) is based upon pp. 318–36 of Paul Peeters' learned article, "La légende de saint Jacques de Nisibe," in *Analecta Bollandiana* 38 (1920), pp. 285–373 ("Invention de l'Arche").

1. The Syrian origin of the legend is indicated by: (a) the discovery of the ark by a Syrian bishop in the Gordian mountains near the Syrian plain; (b) In the "Life of Mar Augin" the legend is placed at Mount Qardu; (c) the earliest reference in Armenian literature is that the ark has been found by a Syrian bishop; (d) early Armenian writers know nothing of Agri Dagi as the landing place.

2. After the legend was translated into Armenian, the landing place was "explained" in two additional ways that introduced confusion. (a) "On the mountains of Ararat" (*i lerins Araraday*: Gen. 8.4) was added. Then, the "s" in *lerins* was accidentally copied at the beginning of the next word, resulting in Sararat. (b) A later copyist, aware of the similarity of the biblical name to the district of Airarat, added the expression, "in the region of Airaratic control."

3. Once this late, edited, confusing Armenian version was understood to refer to the province of Airarat, it was natural for the landing place to be sought nearby. But Agri Dagi was not the only and perhaps not the earliest candidate! Vincent of Beauvais, in the thirteenth century, places St. Jacob's adventure on Mt. Arach, likely the modern Ala-Göz.

Notes

Chapter 1

1. For a discussion of the term "Masis" and the various other designations of the mountain, see P. Gh. Injijian, *Georgraphy of Armenia,* vol. 1, pp. 54 ff. (in Armenian; *nv*). The mountain must not be confused with the Masius Mountains of the classical geographers: a range of 5,000-foot peaks lying south and west of the Tigris, now called Jabal Karaja (Karaga Dag). For the latter, see Heinrich Kiepert, *A Manual of Ancient Geography* (London, 1881), sec. 90, with his *Atlas of Ancient and Classical Geography* (London, 1907), map 19. The similarity of the names may have contributed to the transfer of flood traditions from the area of the Masius range to Masis (see chap. 3).

Chapter 2

1. In general, see Boris Piotrovsky, *The Ancient Civilization of Urartu* (New York, 1969); Charles Burney and David Lang, *The Peoples of the Hills* (New York, 1972).

2. So Herodotus in his *Histories* 7.73. See, however, Burney and Lang, *Peoples,* pp. 177-79, who suggest a connection with the Hurrians.

3. The linguistic phenomenon involved is either an interchange of the consonants *r* and *l* (attested in various languages, particularly Semitic) or an inability to distinguish the two (as in the *lingua franca* of the times, Achaemenian Persian). See George Rowlinson, *History of Herodotus,* 4 vols. (London, 1875), vol. 4, 245 ff. ("On the Alarodians of Herodotus").

4. *Ibid.*; Burney and Lang, *Peoples,* pp. 177-78; H. Kiepert, *A Manual of Ancient Geography,* p. 49.

5. Herodotus 3. 89-94.

6. Kevork Aslan, *Armenia and the Armenians* (New York, 1920), p. 30.

Where is Noah's Ark?

7. Jerome, *Corpus Christianorum: Series Latina* 73.442.

8. Thus the Septuagint (Greek) translation of Isa. 37:38 and the Vulgate (Latin) translation at Gen. 8:4; II Kings 19:37.

9. Kiepert, *Manual*, secs. 40-49; H. F. Tozer, *A History of Ancient Geography* (Cambridge, 1935), pp. 113-14.

10. For later uses of the term "Armenia," in even wider senses, see "Armenia" in *Encyclopaedia Judaica* (1971), vol. 3, 472-75; for the province of Arminiyah during the Abbasid period, see G. Le Strange, *The Lands of the Eastern Caliphate* (Cambridge, 1930), pp. 182-84 (with his map 1).

Chapter 3

1. Collections of sources include: Samuel Bochart, *Geographia sacra: Phaleg et Canaan* (1707), vol. 1, pp. 13-21; J. A. Fabricius, *Codex Pseudepigraphus Veteris Testamentii*, 2 vols. Hamburg and Leipzig, 1713-1733), vol. 1, sec. 33 ("Reliquiae Arcae Noae," (n.v.); Theodor Nöldeke, "Kardu and Kurden," in *Beitrage zur Alten Geschichte und Geographie*, Festschrift für Heinrich Kiepert (Berlin, 1898), p. 73; Louis Ginzberg, *The Legends of the Jews*, 7 vols. (Philadelphia, 1946-1947), vol. 5, p. 186, n. 48; "Deluge," in James Hastings, ed., *Encyclopedia of Religion and Ethics* (Edinburgh, 1911), vol. 4, esp. pp. 553-55; Theodor Nöldeke, "Der Landungspunkt Noahs," in his *Unterzuchungen zur Kritik des Alten Testaments* (Kiel, 1896), pp. 145-55. Much more convenient for the average reader (though rather uncritical at points and slanted toward an identification of the biblical Ararat with Buyuk Agri Dagi) is the limited collection, in English translation, by James W. Montgomery, *The Quest for Noah's Ark*, 2nd ed. (Minneapolis, 1974), pp. 61-98, 325-27. Also: S. C. Malan, *The Book of Adam and Eve* (London, 1882), pp. 239-42.

2. Yakut, *Mu'jam al-Buldan*, vol. 2, p. 270. 11. For other classical sources, see M. Streck, "Djudi," in *Encyclopedia of Islam*, new ed. (1965), vol. 2, pp. 573-74. The precise location of the range is: 27°30'N, 41°30'E. For a description of the area, see William Palgrave, *Narrative of . . . Central and Eastern Arabia* (London, 1865), vol. 1, chap. 3. For a photo, see Alois Musil, *Northern Neğd* (New York, 1928), p. 147.

3. Regis Blanchère, *Dictionnaire Arabe-Francais-Anglais* (Paris: G.-P. Maisonneuve et Larose, 1967-), vol. 3,

1890–1891; "Taiy," in *Encyc. of Islam*, vol. 4 (1934), p. 624a. The deity was apparently named Fals/Fils/Fuls.

4. *Ad Autolycus*, vol. 3, chap. 19 = ANF 2.117.

5. S. Baring-Gould, *Legends of the Patriarchs and Prophets* (New York, 1885), pp. 142-43. I have not been able to find a published account of Prevoux's travels. Presumably, however, his Chenna is the small oasis village of Qanā (sometimes spelled Kenah by western travelers, e.g., Palgrave, *Narrative*, vol. 1, p. 100), just north of the 'Aja' Range (specifically, at 27°47'N, 41°25'E), and thus within sight of the ark's landing place. However, the Department of Antiquities of the Kingdom of Saudi Arabia has informed me that they have no knowledge of this relic at present.

6. Nicholas of Damascus, (first century B.C.), quoted by Josephus, *Antiquities* 1.3.6 = Loeb Classical Library 1.95.

7. The traditional identification with the Minni of Jer. 51:27, mentioned along with the Kingdom of Ararat, seems doubtful on linguistic grounds (so I. J. Gelb, "Minni," in *The Interpreter's Dictionary of the Bible (IDB)* [Nashville: 1962]).

8. Compare Greek βαρις, "tower, elevation"; Persian *barz, burz,* "height, tall"; Old Persian *hara berezaiti,* "high mountain"; Arabic *baraza,* "to come into view, tower up" (said of mountains), *barz,* "hill" (hence: *al-barz,* "the elevation"). See F. Steingass, *A Comprehensive Persian-English Dictionary,* p. 173. col. 2; "Albruz" in *Encyc. of Islam,* new ed.; Le Strange, *Lands,* p. 368, n. One must not confuse Mount Elbruz with the Elburz Mountains in northern Iran. (For the suggestion that Baris means "exit," and is to be connected with Noah's departure from the ark, see Samuel Bochart, *Geographia sacra: Phaleg et Canaan* (1707), p. 20 (1.3). For the Caucasus Range as the ark's landing place, see Th. Gaster, *Myth, Legend, and Custom in the Old Testament,* p. 129. It should also be noted that βαρις can mean "boat," which, while interesting, seems improbable as a basis for naming the mountain; cf., however, Κιβωτός ["box, boat"] as a city name in site no. 4 below.)

9. Carveth Wells, *Kapoot* (New York, 1933), p. 219.

10. This carra (Κάρραι) is often considered to be too far to the southeast to be the famous city of Harran (Χαρραν; Καρρα). The text is often emended to Gordyene (Καρδου; see the Loeb ed.), an area mentioned in other ancient sources as the ark's landing place (see 3b).

Where is Noah's Ark?

11. Josephus, *Antiq.* 20.2.2 (Loeb ed. 20.24-25).

12. Hippolytus, *Refutation of All Heresies* 10, chap. 26 = ANF 5, 149.

13. Julius Africanus, *Fragments . . . of the Chronography* 4 = ANF 6, 131. Parthia was generally to the east of Mesopotamia, but occasionally extended its influence to the area of Greater Armenia. Thus Julius' reference allows for a number of possibilities.

14. Located at 35°45'N, 45°15'E; 8,600 feet tall, snow-capped, and visible for a hundred miles. For the general geography in Assyrian sources, see Maximilian Strech, "Armenien, Kurdistan und Westpersien n.d. Keilinschriften," *ZA* 15 (1900), 257-382 (esp. pp. 272 ff.). For the specific identification of Mt. Nisir and discussion of the area, see E. A. Speiser, "Southern Kurdistan," *AASOR* 8 (1926/27), 1-42 (at pp. 17-18). For a photo, see C. J. Edmonds, *Kurds, Turks, and Arabs* (London, 1957), frontispiece.

15. Strabo,*Geography* 16.1.24=Loeb ed. 7, 231.

16. Xenophon, *Anabasis* 4: Καρδούχοι.

17. Ptolemy, *Geography* 5.13.5; Müller ed., 5.12.2: τὰ Γορδυαῖα ὄρη.

18. E.g., *Ber. Rab.* 33.4 (Albeck ed., vol. 1, p. 309); *Tan.* B, I.41; and the Syriac sources cited under site 5.

19. Josephus, *Antiq.* 1.3.6 = Loeb ed., 1.93; see also *Against Apion,* I.19. Berossus is also quoted in this regard by Eusebius of Caesarea (*Praep. Evang.* 9.12). For general bibliography, see Montgomery, *Quest,* pp. 61-64.

20. Pliny, *Natural History* 6.16.

21. Epiphanius, *Panarion Haer.* 1.1.4 (*Epiphanii Episcopi Constantiae Opera,* ed. G. Dindorfius, vol. 1 [Leipzig, 1859], p. 283 = K. Holl, *Epiphanius,* vol. 1, *Panarion, GCS,* Leipzig, 1915, p. 174): ἀνὰ μέσον 'Αρμενίων Καὶ Καρδυέων.

22. Epiphanius, Dindorfius, ed., vol. 1, p. 324 = Holl, ed., p. 217 (= *Panarion Haer.,* 18.3.4).

23. L. W. King, "Sennacherib and the Ionians," *Journal of Hellenic Studies* 30 (1910), 327-35, at p. 328, n. 2.

24. *Ibid.*; for photos, see Gertrude Bell, *Amurath to Amurath* (London, 1911), p. 290.

25. Bell, *Amurath,* p. 292; "Djudi," in *Encyc. of Islam,* new ed., for sources.

26. *Encyc. of Islam,* "Djudi," new ed., for sources.

112

27. An idea as old as Bochart, *Geographia sacra* (1707), vol. 1, 3 (p. 18).

28. *Encyc. of Islam*, "Djudi", new ed., see also Arthur Jeffrey, *Foreign Vocabulary of the Quran* (Baroda, 1938), p. 107.

29. *Nazm al-jawhir*, p. 41 = Migne, *Patrologiae Cursus Completus* (PCC), 111.915.40.

30. *Murūj al-Dhahab*, chap. 3; trans. B. Meynard and P. Courteille, *Les Prairies d'Or*, vol. 1, p. 74.

31. A. Asher, ed., *The Itinerary of Rabbi Benjamin of Tudela*, vol. 1, pp. 90-91.

32. *al-Madjmu' al-Mubārak*; ed. and trans. Th. Erpenius, *Historica Saracenica . . . a Georgio Elmacino*, vol. 1, p. 17, as quoted by Montgomery, *Quest*, p. 327.

33. *'Adjā'ib al-Makhlūkāt wa-Gharā'ib al-Mawdjūdāt;* ed. Wüstenfeld, *Kosmographie*, vol. 1, p. 156.

34. Eutychius, *Nazm al-jawhir*, p. 43 = Migne, *PCC* 111.915.41-43.

35. Ibn-Hawqal, *al-Masālik w-al-Mamālik*, in the tenth century. Quoted in Montgomery, *Quest*, p. 327.

36. Bell, *Amurath*, p. 293; *Encyc. of Islam*, new ed., "Djudi."

37. Bell, *Amurath*, pp. 289-95; W. F. Ainsworth, *Travels in the Track of the Ten Thousand Greeks* (London, 1844) *n.v.* For a photo, see Bell *Amurath*, p. 291.

38. Bell, *ibid.*, p. 292; and esp. W. A. Wigram and Edgar T. A. Wigram, *The Cradle of Mankind* (London, 1914), pp. 335-36.

39. Sibyline Oracles 1.320 ff. The site is actually at the headwaters of the river Maeander, of which the Marsyas is a tributary.

40. For references in classical sources and for a description of the area, see J. A. Cramer, *A Georgraphical and Historical Description of Asia Minor* (Amsterdam, 1971), vol. 2, pp. 47-52.

41. Cramer, *ibid.*, p. 50; considers the name to be "attached to Apamea probably as a distinctive appellation from the Syrian town of the same name," but he is uncertain as to its meaning.

42. A variety of such traditions are mentioned by James Bryce, *Transcaucasia and Ararat* (London, 1896), pp. 214, 222-24.

43. Josephus, *Antiq.* I.3.v.

44. Ptolemy, *Geography* V.13, xii.

45. Victor Langlois, *Collections des Historiens anciens et modernes de l'Arménie*, 2 vols. (Paris, 1867–1869), vol. 2, p. 242 *b*, n.1; p. 328*b*, n.2.

46. Moses, *History of the Armenians* (Venice, 1881; in Armenian, n.v.); Latin trans. W. and G. Whiston, *Mosis Chorenensis Historia Armeniae* (London, 1736; not widely available in the U.S.; n.v.); French trans. in Langlois, *Collectious*, vol. 2, pp. 53-175. For a brief discussion of his career and works (with dated bibliography), see "Moses (5) of Khoren" in the *Dictionary of Christian Biography*, ed. William Smith and Henry Wace (London, 1882), vol. 3, pp. 949-50. Langlois' index does not contain an entry "Idsheuan" and at vol. 2, 242 *b*, n.1 he points out that the city of Idchavan (= Idsheuan?) in the Province of Airarat is mentioned only by Vartabed.

47. For the beginnings of the debate, see A. Carrière, *Moïse de Khoren et les généalogies patriarcales* (1891, n.v.), and *Nouvelles Sources de Moïse de Khoren* (1893, n.v.), proposing an eighth-century date. The traditional date is defended by F. Conybeare, "The Date of Moses of Khoren," *Byz. Zeitschr.* 10 (1901), 489-504.

48. See in particular, Hans Lewy, "The Date and Purpose of Moses of Chorene's History," *Byzantion* 11 (1936), 81-96, with a rejoinder (to Adontz) at pp. 593-96. His ninth-century date for Moses is challenged in favor of the eighth by N. Adontz, "Sur la Date de l'Histoire de l'Arménie," *ibid.*, pp. 97-100, with a rejoinder (to Lewy) at pp. 597-99. For more recent affirmation of a late ninth-century date, see the literature cited in Berthold Altaner, *Patrology* (1960), p. 411. See also Cyril Toumanoff, *Studies in Christian Caucasian History* (Georgetown, 1963), pp. 330-34, who gives nine reasons for assigning the work to the late eighth century.

49. E.g., while Montgomery (*Quest*, p. 66 note) is happy to quote the remark in the *Oxford Dictionary of the Christian Church*, ed. F. L. Cross, 2nd ed. (London, 1974), p. 944, that Moses' *History* "remains a work of the first importance for the primitive history of Armenia," he has neglected to report that this was prefaced by, ". . . though its contents seem much less reliable than older scholars used to suppose, it . . ."

50. Faustus, *History of the Armenians* (Venice, 1933; in Armenian, n.v.); French trans. in Langlois, *Collections*, vol. 1, pp. 209-310.

51. Usually considered a scribal error for "Ararat" (Lan-

glois, *Collections*, vol. 1, p. 218, n.2). See also Appendix, I and II.

52. An English trans. of the entire passage may be found in Montgomery, *Quest*, pp. 71-74.

53. Langlois, *Collections*, vol. 1, p. 288, nn. 1-2; vol. 2, p. 107*b*, n.4. For a detailed study of the various provinces and the cantons of each, see Heinrich Hübschmann, "Die altarmenischen Ortsnamen," in *Indogermanische Forschungen* 16 (1904), 197-490. A summary account may be found in his *Armenische Grammatik* (Hildesheim, 1962; reprint of the Leipzig ed. of 1897), pp. 403-4, 518-20.

54. Study of the provinces in Armenia is complicated by the fact there have been several systems of boundaries and of designations: those of the Arsacid monarchs; those of the Byzantines, with a revision by Justinian; and those of the Muslims. See briefly, "Arminiya," in *Encyc. of Islam*, new ed. ("Divisions"); H. Gelzer, *Die Genesis der byzantinischen Themenverfassung* (Amsterdam: Adolph Hakkert, 1966), esp. pp. 64-72; and the works of Hübschmann cited in the previous note.

55. For the sources, see "Kurds" in *Encyc. of Islam*.

56. Ptolemy, *Geography*, Müller ed., 5.12.2,3.

57. *Quest*, p. 71, n.3, following Langlois, *Collections*, vol. 2, p. 107*b*, n.4; vol. 1, p. 288, nn.1-2, who is following Saint-Martin, *Memoirs*, vol. 1, p. 176 n.v.).

58. I have used Mühler's text.

59. In the type-font of some Renaissance Latin editions of Ptolemy, an *i* can easily be mistakenly read for a *t*.

60. Κορυαλα in the Greek original: 5. 12. 8 in Mühler but 5. 13. 18 in some others.

61. Κωραλα in the Greek original: 5.12.9 in Mühler but 5.13.20 in some others. For the erroneous Latin reading "Cortaea," on which Montgomery has depended, see Mühler's ed. 1. 2. 947 note.

62. Bell, *Amurath*, p. 294.

63. (a) "Hyms on Paradise," I. 10 [*Ephraem Syrus* (trans. by Renè Lavenant; Paris, 1968), p. 39; *Corpus Scriptorum Christianorum Orientalium* 174. *Scriptores Syri* 78: *Des Heiligen Ephraem des Syrers* (Louvain, 1957), with trans. in vol. 79, p. 3]; (b) "Commentary on Genesis and Exodus," sec. 6, p. 12 [*CSCO* 152, *SS* 71: *Sancti Ephraem Syri* (ed. R.-M. Tonneau; Louvain, 1955), with trans. in vol. 72, p. 48]; (c) "Passover Hyms," VII. 7

[*CSCO* 248, *SS* 108: *Des Heiligen Ephraem des Syrers*, with trans. in vol. 109, p. 57].

64. Cited in Malan, *Adam and Eve*, p. 239, n. 17, citing the Arabic text (in contrast to the Syriac, which places the landing site at Apamea, near Celaenae [site no. 4]. Most of Bar Hebraeus is yet unpublished.

65. For the complete text, see Montgomery, *Quest*, pp. 80-81.

66. S. C. Malan, *The Life and Times of S. Gregory the Illuminator* (London, 1868).

67. "Jacobus (4) or James," in *A Dictionary of Christian Biography*, ed. William Smith and Henry Wace (London, 1882), III, 325-27, at p. 326*b*.

68. Le Strange, *Lands*, p. 94.

69. Trans. in Montgomery, *Quest*, pp. 85-86. "Cemanum" appears to be a corruption of the Hebrew word for "eighty" (*shemōnīm*; Syriac: *themānīn*; Arabic: *thamānīn*).

70. Le Strange, *Lands*, p. 98.

71. Bell, *Amurath*, pp. 291-93.

72. Bryce, *Transcaucasia*, p. 222; Bell, *Amurath*, p. 294.

73. E.g., Sepher Noah, 155, beginning.

74. For the texts, see Hermann Rönsch, *Das Buch der Jubiläen* (Leipzig, 1874), p. 293 (Syncellus, *Chronicle*), p. 305 (Cedrenus, *Synopsis*).

75. Th. Gaster, *Myth, Legend, and Custom in the Old Testament* (New York, 1969), p. 359; Umberto Cassuto, *Genesis*, p. 105; Bochart, *Geographia sacra*, vol. 1, sec. 3, p. 21.

76. For the Islamic traditions, see "Ceylon" in *Encyc. of Islam*.

77. See "Alwand Kuh" in *Encyc. of Islam*, new ed.

78. William Foster, ed., *Thomas Herbert: Travels in Persia, 1627–1629* (London, 1928), pp. 191, 322.

79. C. P. Tiele and W. H. Kosters, "Ararat" in *Encyclopaedia Biblica*, ed. T. K. Cheyne and J. S. Block, 4 vols. (New York, 1899–1903).

80. For a summary of the position, as contained in Lenormant, *Les origines de l'histoire*, vol. 2, pp. 1-45, and for a brief refutation, see J. van den Gheyn, "Ararat," in *Dictionnaire de la Bible* (1895).

81. Tim Le Haye and John Morris, *The Ark of Ararat* (Nashville, 1976), p. 41.

Chapter 4

1. Bryce, *Transcaucasia*, p. 250, relates the story of the Persian Shah who offered a vast reward for anyone able to reach the top. No one claimed it.

2. For the full accounts, see Montgomery, *Quest* pp. 82-83, 85-86, 99-100, 106-9.

3. *Ibid.*, p. 110.

4. J. J. Friedrich Parrot, *Journey to Ararat* (New York, 1855), is a detailed, careful study of the mountain and its surroundings. For a lengthy bibliography of travel in the area and of its topography, see H. F. B. Lynch, *Armenia* (London, 1901), vol. 2, pp. 471-84. Lynch's work is itself a reliable source of information, and is not focused on the search for Noah's ark.

5. For a description of the 1840 eruption that blew away a vast strip of the mountain and created the Ahora Gorge, see Parrot, *Journey*, pp. 385-89.

6. La Haye and Morris, *The Ark of Ararat*, pp. xi-xii, 56 ff.

7. *Ibid.*, pp. 43-49.

8. Montgomery, *Quest*, pp. 158-80 for Stuart's own account. See also Rene Noorbergen, *The Ark File* (Mountain View, Calif., 1974), pp. 106-7, who mentions another expedition in the same time period.

9. Noorbergen, *Ark File*, p. 106, cites the death certificate. Williams' account puts the death in 1918, apparently in error.

10. Bryce, *Transcaucasia*, p. 280.

11. *Ibid.*, p. 281.

12. La Haye and Morris, *Ark on Ararat*, pp. 56-63.

13. Bryce, *Transcaucasia*, pp. 240-44; Lynch, *Armenia*, I, p. 161 (mentions the unique stand of birches on Little Ararat); Balsiger and Sellier, *In Search of Noah's Ark* (Los Angeles, 1976), p. 71.

14. Bryce, *Transcaucasia*, pp. 240-44; Lynch, *Armenia*, p. 167 does mention a seasonal stream near the foot of the mountain, as does Parrot, *Journey*, p. 240.

15. Noorbergen, *Ark File*, pp. 107-8.

16. La Haye and Morris, *Ark on Ararat*, pp. 64-67; Montgomery, *Quest*, pp. 110-12.

17. For considerable detail, see Noorbergen, *Ark File*, pp. 96-102.

18. La Haye and Morris, *Ark on Ararat*, pp. 65-66.

Where is Noah's Ark?

19. For a scholarly discussion, see "Weights and Measures" in *The Interpreter's Dictionary of the Bible*, IV, pp. 836-37. Ark-searchers La Haye and Morris, *Ark on Ararat*, p. 244, list estimates from 17.5 to 24 inches, and prefer ca. 18 inches.

20. Noorbergen, *Ark File*, pp. 99-100.

21. This is the date given in Montgomery, *Quest*, p. 113, who seems to be discussing Hagopian under the assumed name George Tamisian. La Haye and Morris, however, list the date as 1908–1910: *Ark of Ararat*, p. 68. For a long interview with Hagopian, see Noorbergen, *Ark File*, pp. 164-71.

22. La Haye and Morris, *Ark on Ararat*, pp. 73-92; Montgomery, *Quest*, pp. 119-25; Noorbergen, *Ark File*, pp. 82-96.

23. La Haye and Morris, *Ark on Ararat*, pp. 98-101; Montgomery, *Quest*, pp. 125-28.

24. For details, see La Haye and Morris, *Ark on Ararat*, pp. 115-25.

25. A Kurd named Shukru Asena from the vicinity of Buyuk Agri Dagi is reported to have given the story to reporter Edwin Greenwald in Istanbul, Turkey. However, the subject indexes for 1948 of the *New York Times* and of the *London Times* indicate that they did not carry the item, which La Haye and Morris, *Ark on Ararat* date to Nov. 13.

26. Smith reportedly published two books on the topic: *The Reported Discovery of Noah's Ark* (Orlando, Fla.: Christ for the World Publishers, 1949); *On the Mountains of Ararat in Quest of Noah's Ark* (Apollo, Pa., 1950). Cited by La Haye and Morris, *Ark of Ararat*, p. 125 nn. 1-2.

27. Balsiger and Sellier, *In Search*, pp. 159-60.

Chapter 5

1. It is sometimes claimed that various aviators saw or photographed the ark, and that an edition of *Stars and Stripes* in 1943 carried an article about some of them. To date, however, it appears that neither airman, nor newspaper, nor photo has been produced as evidence. See La Haye and Morris, *The Ark on Ararat*, pp. 103-7; Dave Balsiger and Charles Sellier, *In Search*, pp. 155-57.

2. For discussion, see Montgomery, *Quest*, pp. 128-31, 252-53; Balsiger and Sellier, *In Search*, pp. 160-61. For a sketch based upon the photos, see Montgomery, following p. 192.

3. See "Noah's Ark?" *Life Magazine,* Sept. 5, 1960, pp. 112-14. For discussion, see La Haye and Morris, *Ark on Ararat,* pp. 143-44. For a copy of the photo, see Balsiger and Sellier, *In Search,* following p. 106. For a detailed account by a member of the expedition, see Noorbergen, *Ark File,* chap. 5.

4. For a copy of the photo, see Balsiger and Sellier, *In Search,* following p. 106, with discussion at pp. 164-65; La Haye and Morris, *Ark on Ararat,* pp. 176-78 (with photo on p. 177).

5. La Haye and Morris, *Ark on Ararat,* p. 177 (Morris was a member of the ICR group that tried to locate the object).

6. *Ibid.*

7. For a copy, see *ibid.,* p. 204 (with a wider area photographed from Skylab on p. 202); Montgomery, *Quest,* following p. 192 (two photos, one magnified).

8. Balsiger and Sellier, *In Search,* pp. 192-96.

9. Montgomery's own account is found in *Quest,* pp. 316-17, with copies of the correspondence involved at pp. 350-55.

10. *Ibid.,* pp. 355-56; La Haye and Morris, *Ark on Ararat,* pp. 203-5.

11. For the problem, see chap. 4, n.19.

12. As quoted in La Haye and Morris, *Ark on Ararat,* pp. 205-7; Balsiger and Sellier, *In Search,* pp. 194-96.

13. Montgomery, *Quest,* p. 317.

14. For discussion, see La Haye and Morris, *Ark on Ararat,* pp. 190, 214-15. For a copy of the photo, see Balsiger and Sellier, *In Search,* following p. 106.

15. La Haye and Morris, *Ark on Ararat,* pp. 214-15. Balsiger and Sellier are more cautious; *In Search,* p. 163.

16. La Haye and Morris, *Ark on Ararat,* p. 215.

Chapter 6

1. It was viewing this relic that helped encourage Navarra to journey to the mountain: Balsiger and Sellier, *In Search,* p. 167.

2. See his account in *Noah's Ark: I Touched It* (Plainfield, 1974), pp. 49-69, with abundant photos. However, the exact location of the "find" is unclear. Navarra allegedly indicated three different spots, several thousand feet apart.

Where is Noah's Ark?

See Noorbergen, *Ark File*, pp. 162-63, with the map on p. 155.

3. For copies of their reports, see Navarra, *Noah's Ark*, pp. 125-32.

4. Such chronological reckoning bristles with difficulties, and there are major tensions between the manuscript families (e.g., MT and LXX). See "Chronology, OT," in *The Interpreter's Dictionary of the Bible* and *IDBS, Supplementary Volume.*

5. *New York Times*, Feb. 27, 1970, p. 39; Mar. 1, 1970, sec. IV, p. 8. For Navarra's diary account, see *Noah's Ark*, pp. 70-94.

6. *Radiocarbon*, VII (1965), 161. The report concludes with the comment: "Evidently not the ark."

7. Radiocarbon dates traditionally have been based upon a 5568 half-life for C^{14}, but this has recently been revised to 5730. A 5568-derived age multiplied by 1.03 yields a 5730-derived age. In either case, the age of the sample is substracted from 1950 to give the before-present date. "Correction" is an adjustment based upon C^{14} dating of tree-ring dated samples (see below). The "corrections" given in this article are courtesy of the University of Pennsylvania; e.g., the 1190 age multiplied by 1.03 equals 1225; A.D. 1950 minus 1225 equals A.D. 725. But with a fifty-year "correction" substracted, we get: 1225-50=1175; 1950-1175=A.D. 775.

8. *Science News* 111, Mar, 26, 1977, 198-99. I have confirmed this by telephone conversation with the director of the laboratory, Professor Rainer Berger. Results will be published as "UCLA Radiocarbon Dates X," in a future issue of *Radiocarbon*.

9. *Ibid.*; confirmed by telephone conversation with Professor R. E. Taylor, Deptartment of Anthropology. He and Professor Berger are preparing an article that will examine all the radiocarbon evidence in this matter.

10. Radiocarbon laboratories file test results under a specimen number and under the name of the person who submitted the specimen for analysis (rather than by the location where it was found). This has made retrieval of test results somewhat difficult for me.

11. *Science News* 97 June 13, 1970, 574, discussing only tests allegedly done at Geochron, University of Pennsylvania, and UCLA. I have not discovered any support for the claim in *Christianity Today* 13, Sept. 12, 1969, 48)

that the wood has been radiocarbon dated to 4,000 years of age. The publisher's foreword to Navarra, *Noah's Ark* (p. xi) lists an age of 1,500 years but does not identify the lab. Page 136 alludes to a radiocarbon age of 4,448 years, but gives no documentation to support it. See Noorbergen, *Ark File*, pp. 135-37, 143, for reasons to doubt that such a test was ever done. Listing Navarra's book as his source, William Stiebing (in *The Biblical Archaeology Review* 2, no. 2, p. 17) gives a range of 450-750 A.D. (Thus one can scarcely believe anything concerning this topic that has been published in popular works.)

12. Noorbergen, *Ark File*, p. 142. Confirmed by telephone by the laboratory director, Harold Krueger. The specimen number is Gx 1668.

13. *Science News* 97, no. 24; Balsiger and Sellier, *In Search*, pp. 185-86; *New York Times*, Feb. 27, 1970, p. 39.

14. This result will be published in *Radiocarbon* (probably vol. 19). It is quoted here with the kind permission of the university's Radiocarbon Laboratory, granted by Ms. Barbara Lawn.

15. Noorbergen, *Ark File*, p. 142, identified by the laboratory director as Gx 1667.

16. E.g., Navarra's book makes no mention of them (in contrast to a brief note in the publisher's foreword).

17. Montgomery (*Quest*, p. 255) speaks only of "widely divergent results", La Haye and Morris (*Ark on Ararat*, p. 132) say that the (unspecified) results "far exceed a proper percentage of error."

18. Cited in *New York Times*, Mar. 1, 1970, Sect. IV, p. 8, concerning the 1969 wood.

19. For reasonably informed but dated objections to the method in general (from the point of view of someone sympathetic to biblical chronology, and generally in polemical tones), see John Whitcomb, Jr., and Henry Morris, *The Genesis Flood* (Philadelphia, 1961), pp. 370-79. For detailed up-to-date discussion of the limitations of the method, by radiocarbon scientists, see Ingrid Olsson, *Radiocarbon Variations and Absolute Chronology*, Nobel Symposium 12 (New York, 1970); see also the review by Robert Adams in *JNES* 32 (1973), 253-56. For an excellent general discussion, see J. O. D. Johnston, "The Problems of Radiocarbon Dating," *PEQ* (1973), 13-26.

20. In addition to the sources cited in note 19, see Balsiger and Sellier, *In Search*, p. 190.

Where is Noah's Ark?

21. Olsson, *Radiocarbon Variations*, p. 305.

22. Navarra, *Noah's Ark*, p. 124.

23. So the caption beneath one of the pictures in *Noah's Ark* (following p. 76, on the 4th photo page). However, the caption under the 6th photo page speaks of "the three pieces . . . refitted," as does the text on p. 63 (thus one can scarcely trust even the most elemental statements about this entire matter). To make matters worse, the beam as reconstructed (photos above) bears striking dissimilarities to what is allegedly the same beam still intact atop the mountain (*Noah's Ark*, following p. 76, photo pp. 2-3). This may be due, however, to the perspective from which the various photos were taken, or to Navarra's chopping activity.

24. La Haye and Morris, *Ark on Ararat*, p. 132.

25. *Science News* 111, Mar. 26, 1977, p. 198, citing research done at the University of California, La Jolla, by Professor Hans Suess.

26. La Haye and Morris, *Ark on Ararat*, p. 132; Balsiger and Sellier, *In Search*, p. 189

27. *Science News* 111, pp. 198-99.

28. In general, see H. E. Suess, "The Three Causes of the Secular C^{14} Fluctuations," in Olsson, ed., *Radiocarbon Variations*, pp. 595-605.

29. R. E. Lingenfelter and R. Ramaty, "Astrophysical and Geophysical Variations in C^{14} Productions," in *ibid.*, pp. 513-37.

30. V. Bucha, "Influence of the Earth's Magnetic Field on Radiocarbon Dating," in *ibid.*, pp. 501-11.

31. J. Labeyrie, G. Delibrias, and J. C. Duplessy, "The Possible Origin of Natural Carbon Radioactivity Fluctuations in the Past," in *ibid.*, 539-47.

32. J. C. Lerman, W. G. Mook, and J. C. Vogel, "C^{14} in Tree Rings from Different Localities," in *ibid.*, pp. 275-301, esp. pp. 292-97.

33. See the series of articles under the heading, "C^{14} and Dendrochronology," in *ibid.*, pp. 233-333.

34. *Ibid.*; H. N. Michael and E. K. Ralph, "Correction Factors Applied to Egyptian Radiocarbon Dates from the Era before Christ," *ibid.*, pp. 109-20 (with various charts, including plate 2); E. K. Ralph, H. N. Michael, and M. C. Han, "Radiocarbon Dates and Reality," *MASCA Newsletter* 9, August, 1973.

35. See Balsiger and Sellier, *In Search*, p. 189, who claim even more excessive variations.

36. As do La Haye and Morris, *Ark on Ararat*, pp. 132-33.

37. See the series of articles under the heading "C14 and Archaeology" in Olsson, *Radiocarbon Variations*, pp. 23-126.

38. W. S. Glock and S. Agerter, "Anomalous Patterns in Tree Rings," *Endeavor* 22 (1963), 9-13.

39. C. W. Ferguson, "Bristlecone Pine: Science and Esthetics," *Science* 159 (1968), 839-46, at p. 840.

40. Navarra, *Noah's Ark*, pp. 125-28.

41. *Ibid.*, pp. 128-32.

42. Balsiger and Sellier, *In Search*, p. 185.

43. *Noah's Ark*, pp. 132-33.

44. Balsiger and Sellier, *In Search*, p. 185.

45. So also *ibid.*, p. 181.

46. This seems to refer to lignite formation and not lignin loss. Navarra's documents make no mention of this.

47. Presumably, degradation is meant.

48. See, e.g., Richard Leo and Elso Barghoorn, "Silicification of Wood," *Harvard Museum Leaflets* 25, Dec. 7, 1976, 4.

49. Personal communication from palaeobotanists at North Carolina State University.

50. Leo and Barghoorn in *Harvard Museum Leaflets* 25, p. 27.

51. Letter to the University of Pennsylvania Radiocarbon lab, as quoted in Noorbergen, *Ark File*, p. 143.

52. $\frac{.175}{.275} = \frac{X}{5000}.$ If Bordeaux's alternative identification is adopted *(Quercus castaneifolia)*, the age becomes less still: 2,950 years.

53. Navarra, *Noah's Ark*, pp. 126-27.

54. Written by Professor A. C. Barefoot and dated June 15, 1977.

55. "Noah's Ark Goes to Hollywood," in ICR Impact Series, No. 47, (May, 1977), p. iv.

56. *Journey to Ararat*, pp. 167, 172, 174-75 187, 190, 194-95.

57. Cited in La Haye and Morris, *Ark on Ararat*, p. 54. See Stuart's account of having rediscovered it in 1856 (in Montgomery, *Quest*, p. 178).

58. *Ibid.* Sixty soldiers and loads of scientific equipment accompanied him, and he spent five days atop the mountain. For an account, see Montgomery, *Quest*, pp. 152-57.

59. Montgomery, *Quest*, p. 214.

60. See his account, quoted in La Haye and Morris, *Ark on Ararat*, at p. 24.

61. Jondanus (14th cent.) reports this. See Montgomery, *Quest*, pp. 86-88.

62. This is a cryptic remark, perhaps alluding to the charge, sometimes allegedly made by Navarra's associates, that both the 1955 and the 1969 wood specimens involved "fraud" (La Haye and Morris, *Ark on Ararat*, pp. 133-34, 157-60). See Noorbergen, *Ark File*, pp. 161-62, for another such charge.

63. ICR Impact Series, No. 47, p. iv.

Chapter 7

1. On NBC, May 2 and Dec. 24, 1977.

2. Produced by Charles E. Sellier, Jr., for Sun Classic Pictures, Los Angeles, Calif. It is related to a book by the same title, written by Dave Balsiger and Charles Sellier, Jr. and published by Sun Classic Books Los Angeles, 1976).

3. *Excavations at Ur* (1954). However, Woolley himself did tend to see his discovery as evidence in support of the biblical account. Few subsequent examiners of the evidence have agreed with his interpretation.

4. See the excellent summary in "Flood (Genesis)," *IDB*, s.v. The various silt layers that have been uncovered in excavations in the Near East indicate local floods at widely differing times. For the opinion of a widely respected biblical scholar, see John Bright, "Has Archaeology Found Evidence of the Flood?" in *The Biblical Archaeologist* 4 (Dec., 1942), 55-62. For the geological solutions of a far more "conservative" person (who is not a biblical scholar), see Whitcomb and Morris, *Genesis Flood*.

5. The production notes for the film, entitled *Noah's Ark: The Facts*, contain the following statement: "Ancient accounts report that pilgrims climbed Mt. Ararat as early as 700 B.C. to scrape pitch from a ship believed to be the Ark." However, I am not aware of any statement of the ark's survival from such an early period. Indeed, it seems first to have been reported by Berossus four hundred years later. In any case, there is no reason to believe that such accounts refer to Agri Dagi (see chap. 3).

6. Nineteenth ed. (1951), p. 82.

7. R. Noorbergen, *Ark File*, pp. 135-37.

8. For a brief discussion, see Balsiger and Sellier, *In Search*, pp. 196-98.

9. Ark-searcher John Morris (ICR Impact Series, No. 47, p. iv) claims that the spot of unique reflectivity is indeed the schoolhouse roof, located at 5,000 feet elevation, rather than at 14,000 feet as the movie indicates. However, the spot seems indeed to be at the snow line, and thus Morris' claim would be without foundation. He makes a similarly erroneous claim (p. ii) concerning the location of the object in the ERTS photo which Montgomery initially thought to be the ark (see chap. 5, sect.4).

Chapter 8

1. For the basic story, see *New York Times*, July 19, 1970, p. 11; for speculations as to why permission was refused, see Balsiger and Sellier, *In Search* pp. 205-7; Montgomery, *Quest*, pp. 294-97.

2. For various accounts of difficulties, see Balsiger and Sellier, *In Search*, pp. 70-74; Montgomery, *Quest*, pp. 271-78; La Haye and Morris, *Ark on Ararat*, pp. 180-87.

3. See above, chap. 4, n. 1; Parrot, *Journey to Ararat*, pp. 163-64.

4. *Ibid.*, pp. 199-209.

5. Lynch, *Armenia*, I, 198; Parrot, *Journey*, pp. 171, 219; Bryce, *Transcaucasia*, pp. 239-40.

6. Bryce, *Transcaucasia*, p. 305, 293.

7. Lynch, *Armenia*, vol. 1, pp. 169, 177.

8. *Noah's Ark: I Touched It*, pp. 40-69, with photos.

9. Montgomery, *Quest*, p. 276, with photo following p. 192.

10. Cited by La Haye and Morris, *Ark on Ararat*, p. 70.

11. Parrot, *Journey*, pp. 170-187.

12. An opinion quoted in the *New York Times*, Feb. 27, 1970, p. 39.

13. La Haye and Morris, *Ark on Ararat*, p. 261.

14. For drawings, based upon Assyrian reliefs, see Martin Beek, *Atlas of Mesopotamia* (London, 1962), plates 42-46.

15. Balsiger and Sellier, *In Search*, pp. 122, 184-85.

16. *Encyclopedia Britannica*, 1956 ed., see under "oak."

17. *Flora Orientális* (Geneva, 1879), vol. 4, pp. 1163-64, 1170-71, 1174.

18. See under "Forest," in *IDBS*.

Where is Noah's Ark?

19. See"*Aghri Dagh,*" in *Encyc. of Islam,* new ed., for sources; see also Le Strange, *Lands,* p. 182; for al-Istakhri's text, see M. J. de Goeje, ed., *Bibliotheca Georgraphorum Arabicorum,* vol. 3 (Leiden, 1906).

20. As suggested in the *New York Times,* Mar. 1, 1970, sec. 4, p. 8, and elsewhere.

21. Navarra, *Noah's Ark,* p. 121, for the later date.

22. "The Ark Again?" in *Newsletter Number 3* of the American Schools of Oriental Research (October, 1970).

23. *The Ark File,* pp. 50-53.

24. As quoted in Montgomery, *Quest,* pp. 86-88.

25. Navarra, *Noah's Ark,* p. 124.

26. *Ibid.* p. 128.

27. $\dfrac{(50 \times 10)\,\text{mm}}{2} = 250\,\text{mm radius}; \dfrac{250}{3\,\text{mm average}} = 83.$

28. Balsiger and Sellier, *In Search,* p. 185.

29. $\dfrac{(5\,\text{ft.} \times 12\,\text{in.} \times 2.54\,\text{cm} \times 10)\,\text{mm diameter}}{2 \times 3\,\text{mm average (?)}/\text{annual ring}} = 254\,\text{years.}$

Appendix

1. Compare Müller-Simonis, *Durch Armenien, Kurdistan, und Mesopotamien,* p. 43.

2. Pronounced Nachtschavan, now Nachitschevan on the maps. Designated Ναξονάνα by Ptolemy, located near Armavir and Artašat. A diminutive form is Naxjavanik, a village in the Canton of Khašunikh in the Province of Siunikh (Steph. *Orb.* vol. 2, p. 270).

3. Cf. Injijean, *Storagruthiun him Hayast.* (Venice, 1822), p. 219 (=*nax iǰevan* or *nax avan,* etc.).

4. Cf. *iǰanem,* from *ēǰanem; iǰic,* gen. pl. of *ēǰk'.*

5. Thus in the Moscow ed. 1853, e.g., at pp. 61, 117, 179, along with Naxçavan (var, Naxçuan), p. 56.

6. Thus the Moscow ed. 1860, e.g., p. 265.

7. Cf. Leon Alischan, *Sisakan* (Venice, 1893), p. 497; "The oldest and best authors, [Moses of] Chorene and others, always write [the name as] Naxčavan until approx. 12th and 13th centuries." Cf. also np. Naxčuvān, Naxjuvān, gr. Ναξονάνα (in Ptolemy).

8. Thus L. Alischan, *Sisakan,* p. 497.

9. *I learn Sararaday.* Since Sararad is the mountain itself (see Faustus, p. 24, li. 5 from the bottom; *i Sararad lerinn*), and not the territory in which it lay, it cannot be translated "on the mountain of Sararad" (Murad, p. 71).

With words for province, canton, city, market-town, village, mountain, etc., Armenian usage requires the name either in the genitive case or (esp. when it comes first) uninflected as appositional, e.g., *gavarn Airaratu* (FB, 143; Laz. Pharp., 283), or *Airarat gavarn, gavarin*, etc. (quite often)= "the Province Airarat." Has Sararad evolved from Ararad = Ararat (see below)? Cf. Murad, p. 84, note.

10. This totally unique and far-fetched expression ("region of Airaratic control") has for long been problematic to me (so also for Murad, p. 84). When Faustus elsewhere mentions the Canton of Gordukh (or other canton in Armenia), the phrase "Canton of Gordukh" (or "Canton of Aloyhovit," etc.) always seems a sufficient description to him, with no necessity for more precise designations. Such a designation would be superfluous if it even mentioned that the canton belonged to the country or kingdom of Armenia. This is already sufficiently indicated in the words "in the Armenian Mountains." Moreover, there never was such a thing as Airaratic rule, but rather only control by the Arsacid kings who resided in a city in the Province of Airarat. Faustus uses the phrase only to indicate that if the ark landed in the Canton of Gordukh, it landed, if not in the Province of Airarat, then surely in one of the regions of Armenia ruled by Airarat. Thus, he obviously intends to harmonize the Babylonian-Syrian account with the biblical, as the Jewish tradition had already done when Ararat (Armenian: Airarat) was identified with Qardu (Armenian: Gordukh). (Murad, pp. 26, 39.) The contradiction between the two accounts was later (11th–12th centuries) emphasized by an Armenian writer; however, at the same time, the conflict was decided, naturally, in favor of the Bible (Murad, p. 91). I cannot agree that, in the passage from Faustus, Airarat still had the meaning of the old kingdom of Urartu as preferred by Dr. Belck (verbal communication).

11. Cf. Nöldeke, *Festschrift für Kiepert*, p. 77.

12. Did the Armenian translator of Gen. 8:4 comprehend the meaning of 'Αραράτ? Why did he not more clearly translate it as *Airarat* (as did the translator of Jer. 51:27)? In any case, *Ararat* (var.: *Ararad*) is only the transliteration of Greek 'Αραράτ, and is a thoroughly un-Armenian word by no means derived from *Airarat* (contrary to Murad, p. 20). Just as strange is *Ararad* in the phrase *erkirn Araraday*, "the territory of Ararat": II Kings 19:37;

Where is Noah's Ark?

(Pseudo-)Sebēos (Petersburg, 1879), p. 2; and three times in Moses of Chorene, pp. 22, 23. And Sararad? Cf. Murad, pp. 23, 91-92n., 102.

13. In the Canton of Sasun (Injij., p. 70), west of Lake Van. Moses has selected' this mountain because of the resemblance of its name to the name Sem (the son of Noah), which he here changes to Sim.

14. *i noin getezerbn?* The preposition *i* can only be combined with the dative, accusative, and ablative, but not with the instrumental case.

15. Cf. Murad, pp. 91-92.

16. Ijavank', the name of a village in [the Province of] Airarat (Elišē, [Venice, 1859], p. 139, Murad, p. 63) indeed means "disembark, descend, land": ἀποβαίνειν (from *ijanel*). However, it is located in the Canton of Vanand, far away from Mount Masis, and it has no connection with the flood narrative.